MAKING FRIENDS WITH YO

Overcoming Common Problems Series

For a full list of titles please contact
Sheldon Press, Marylebone Road, London NW1 4DU

Antioxidants
DR ROBERT YOUNGSON

The Assertiveness Workbook
JOANNA GUTMANN

Beating the Comfort Trap
DR WINDY DRYDEN AND JACK GORDON

Body Language
ALLAN PEASE

Body Language in Relationships
DAVID COHEN

Calm Down
DR PAUL HAUCK

Cancer – A Family Affair
NEVILLE SHONE

The Cancer Guide for Men
HELEN BEARE AND NEIL PRIDDY

The Candida Diet Book
KAREN BRODY

Caring for Your Elderly Parent
JULIA BURTON-JONES

Cider Vinegar
MARGARET HILLS

Comfort for Depression
JANET HORWOOD

Considering Adoption?
SARAH BIGGS

Coping Successfully with Hay Fever
DR ROBERT YOUNGSON

Coping Successfully with Pain
NEVILLE SHONE

Coping Successfully with Panic Attacks
SHIRLEY TRICKETT

Coping Successfully with PMS
KAREN EVENNETT

Coping Successfully with Prostate Problems
ROSY REYNOLDS

Coping Successfully with RSI
MAGGIE BLACK AND PENNY GRAY

Coping Successfully with Your Hiatus Hernia
DR TOM SMITH

Coping Successfully with Your Irritable Bladder
DR JENNIFER HUNT

Coping Successfully with Your Irritable Bowel
ROSEMARY NICOL

Coping When Your Child Has Special Needs
SUZANNE ASKHAM

Coping with Anxiety and Depression
SHIRLEY TRICKETT

Coping with Blushing
DR ROBERT EDELMANN

Coping with Bronchitis and Emphysema
DR TOM SMITH

Coping with Candida
SHIRLEY TRICKETT

Coping with Chronic Fatigue
TRUDIE CHALDER

Coping with Coeliac Disease
KAREN BRODY

Coping with Cystitis
CAROLINE CLAYTON

Coping with Depression and Elation
DR PATRICK McKEON

Coping with Eczema
DR ROBERT YOUNGSON

Coping with Endometriosis
JO MEARS

Coping with Epilepsy
FIONA MARSHALL AND DR PAMELA CRAWFORD

Coping with Fibroids
MARY-CLAIRE MASON

Coping with Gallstones
DR JOAN GOMEZ

Coping with Headaches and Migraine
SHIRLEY TRICKETT

Coping with a Hernia
DR DAVID DELVIN

Coping with Psoriasis
PROFESSOR RONALD MARKS

Coping with Rheumatism and Arthritis
DR ROBERT YOUNGSON

Coping with Stammering
TRUDY STEWART AND JACKIE TURNBULL

Coping with Stomach Ulcers
DR TOM SMITH

Overcoming Common Problems Series

Coping with Strokes
DR TOM SMITH

Coping with Thrush
CAROLINE CLAYTON

Coping with Thyroid Problems
DR JOAN GOMEZ

Coping with Your Cervical Smear
KAREN EVENNETT

Crunch Points for Couples
JULIA COLE

Curing Arthritis – The Drug-Free Way
MARGARET HILLS

Curing Arthritis – More ways to a drug-free life
MARGARET HILLS

Curing Arthritis Diet Book
MARGARET HILLS

Curing Arthritis Exercise Book
MARGARET HILLS AND JANET HORWOOD

Cystic Fibrosis – A Family Affair
JANE CHUMBLEY

Depression
DR PAUL HAUCK

Depression at Work
VICKY MAUD

Everything Parents Should Know About Drugs
SARAH LAWSON

Fertility
JULIE REID

Feverfew
DR STEWART JOHNSON

Gambling – A Family Affair
ANGELA WILLANS

Garlic
KAREN EVENNETT

Getting a Good Night's Sleep
FIONA JOHNSTON

The Good Stress Guide
MARY HARTLEY

Heart Attacks – Prevent and Survive
DR TOM SMITH

Helping Children Cope with Attention Deficit Disorder
DR PATRICIA GILBERT

Helping Children Cope with Bullying
SARAH LAWSON

Helping Children Cope with Divorce
ROSEMARY WELLS

Helping Children Cope with Dyslexia
SALLY RAYMOND

Helping Children Cope with Grief
ROSEMARY WELLS

Helping Children Cope with Stammering
JACKIE TURNBULL AND TRUDY STEWART

Hold Your Head Up High
DR PAUL HAUCK

How to Accept Yourself
DR WINDY DRYDEN

How to Be Your Own Best Friend
DR PAUL HAUCK

How to Cope when the Going Gets Tough
DR WINDY DRYDEN AND JACK GORDON

How to Cope with Anaemia
DR JOAN GOMEZ

How to Cope with Bulimia
DR JOAN GOMEZ

How to Cope with Difficult Parents
DR WINDY DRYDEN AND JACK GORDON

How to Cope with Difficult People
ALAN HOUEL WITH CHRISTIAN GODEFROY

How to Cope with People who Drive You Crazy
DR PAUL HAUCK

How to Cope with Stress
DR PETER TYRER

How to Enjoy Your Retirement
VICKY MAUD

How to Get Where You Want to Be
CHRISTIAN GODEFROY

How to Improve Your Confidence
DR KENNETH HAMBLY

How to Interview and Be Interviewed
MICHELE BROWN AND GYLES BRANDRETH

How to Keep Your Cholesterol in Check
DR ROBERT POVEY

How to Love and Be Loved
DR PAUL HAUCK

How to Pass Your Driving Test
DONALD RIDLAND

How to Raise Confident Children
CAROLE BALDOCK

How to Stand up for Yourself
DR PAUL HAUCK

Overcoming Common Problems Series

How to Start a Conversation and Make Friends
DON GABOR

How to Stick to a Diet
DEBORAH STEINBERG AND
DR WINDY DRYDEN

How to Stop Worrying
DR FRANK TALLIS

The How to Study Book
ALAN BROWN

How to Succeed as a Single Parent
CAROLE BALDOCK

How to Untangle Your Emotional Knots
DR WINDY DRYDEN AND JACK GORDON

How to Write a Successful CV
JOANNA GUTMANN

Hysterectomy
SUZIE HAYMAN

The Irritable Bowel Diet Book
ROSEMARY NICOL

The Irritable Bowel Stress Book
ROSEMARY NICOL

Is HRT Right for You?
DR ANNE MACGREGOR

Jealousy
DR PAUL HAUCK

Learning to Live with Multiple Sclerosis
DR ROBERT POVEY, ROBIN DOWIE AND GILLIAN PRETT

Living with Asthma
DR ROBERT YOUNGSON

Living with Crohn's Disease
DR JOAN GOMEZ

Living with Diabetes
DR JOAN GOMEZ

Living with Grief
DR TONY LAKE

Living with High Blood Pressure
DR TOM SMITH

Living with Nut Allergies
KAREN EVENNETT

Living with Osteoporosis
DR JOAN GOMEZ

Living with a Stoma
DR CRAIG WHITE

Motor Neurone Disease – A Family Affair
DR DAVID OLIVER

Overcoming Anger
DR WINDY DRYDEN

Overcoming Anxiety
DR WINDY DRYDEN

Overcoming Guilt
DR WINDY DRYDEN

Overcoming Jealousy
DR WINDY DRYDEN

Overcoming Procrastination
DR WINDY DRYDEN

Overcoming Shame
DR WINDY DRYDEN

Overcoming Your Addictions
DR WINDY DRYDEN AND
DR WALTER MATWEYCHUK

The Parkinson's Disease Handbook
DR RICHARD GODWIN-AUSTEN

The PMS Diet Book
KAREN EVENNETT

A Positive Thought for Every Day
DR WINDY DRYDEN

Rheumatoid Arthritis
MARY-CLAIRE MASON AND
DR ELAINE SMITH

Second Time Around
ANNE LOVELL

Serious Mental Illness – A Family Affair
GWEN HOWE

The Stress Workbook
JOANNA GUTMANN

The Subfertility Handbook
VIRGINIA IRONSIDE AND SARAH BIGGS

Successful Au Pairs
HILLI MATTHEWS

Talking with Confidence
DON GABOR

Ten Steps to Positive Living
DR WINDY DRYDEN

Think Your Way to Happiness
DR WINDY DRYDEN AND JACK GORDON

The Travellers' Good Health Guide
TED LANKESTER

Understanding Obsessions and Compulsions
DR FRANK TALLIS

Understanding Sex and Relationships
ROSEMARY STONES

Understanding Your Personality
PATRICIA HEDGES

Overcoming Common Problems

Making Friends with Your Stepchildren

Rosemary Wells

First published in Great Britain in 2001
Sheldon Press, SPCK, Holy Trinity Church, Marylebone Road, London NW1 4DU

© Rosemary Wells 2001

All rights reserved. No part of this book may be reproduced
or transmitted in any form or by any means, electronic or
mechanical, including photocopying, recording, or by any
information storage and retrieval system, without permission
in writing from the publisher.

British Library Cataloguing-in-Publication Data
A catalogue record for this book is available from the British Library

ISBN 0–85969–846–7

Typeset by Deltatype Limited, Birkenhead, Merseyside
Printed in Great Britain by Biddles Ltd
www.biddles.co.uk

Contents

	Acknowledgements	viii
	Preface	ix
1	Shall We Get Together?	1
2	Consulting the Children	13
3	Endless Complexities	23
4	Settling into the New Family	35
5	Guilt, Jealousy, Resentment and Anger	47
6	Keeping the Peace – Family Rules	59
7	We're All in This Together	71
8	The Extended Stepfamily	83
9	Legal Problems	95
10	The Stepchildren Talk Back	105
	Sources of Help	113
	Further Reading	115
	Index	117

Acknowledgements

I would like to thank the many people who gave so generously of their time, professional advice and helpful comments during my research for this book. Foremost among the therapists, mediators and experts in child welfare to whom I owe a debt of gratitude, I would like to mention Professor Judy Dunn, Miss Melissa Adams, Dr Gwyneth Rees, and Anna Clarke.

My grateful thanks are also due to those organizations that enabled me to study their work among stepfamilies, including: Parentline Plus, the Tavistock Clinic, Relate, Families Need Fathers, and Home Start UK.

My heartfelt thanks also to all the families – parents and children, grandparents and grandchildren – who shared their experiences with me. And to the teachers who willingly discussed their own views and those of their schools.

Last, but not least, very special thanks to Karin Walker, Member of the Solicitors Family Law Association, Family Law Partner and Mediator at Callaghans of Guildford, who generously gave of her time to check the legal content of the book.

Preface

In Britain today there are around 2.5 million children and young adults growing up in stepfamilies, and this does not account for those partners who are cohabiting rather than marrying for a second or subsequent time. And we are told that by the year 2010 there will be more stepfamilies than birth families. Such statistics, quite rightly, engender enormous sympathy for the children who, given little or no choice, have been dumped into new families, new lives, and often new homes and schools too. But their parents should not be forgotten – they also need our sympathy, and possibly our support. Their new role is not a straightforward one – even if it is one of their own choosing. Naturally they love their new partner, but what if that partner brings children along as part of the package? Is it possible to love them also? When such an idea is suggested, stepparents have been known to reply, 'You must be joking!' A wry comment, but an understandable first reaction.

Stepfamilies are born from loss – through death, divorce, or separation. As a stepparent, you cannot ignore the diverse implications of that loss. It is not something that can be left behind when entering a new relationship – especially if there are children involved. No one can just forget the loss of a 20-year marriage, or even a two-year marriage. And, of course, following a loss caused by death, no one even wants to forget.

There are endless variations in step-relationships – from a young girl marrying a widowed father with one baby, to a divorced mother of three forming a relationship with a separated father of two. Each situation requires widely different behaviour. All of which means that the basic ingredient needed when contemplating any such new partnership is a sense of realism. Easy to say – but not easy to grasp if you have fallen hopelessly in love.

'I certainly didn't realize what I was letting myself in for, nobody told me what it would be like.' When working among stepfamilies, I heard such remarks over and over again, and I soon realized that although many families were experiencing highly complex and difficult situations, each one was different. How would it be possible to help them?

I would never presume to give unequivocal advice. However, by letting stepparents and stepchildren tell their own stories in this book, and relate their own experiences, you may discover families who started out with similar problems to your own, and the means they found of managing these difficulties. You will read all their varying comments: 'Never feel it is your duty to love the kids'; 'I love both my stepchildren, it is hard not to when you have brought them up'; 'I certainly feel love for my stepson, but it is a different love, just as you have a different love for all the people in your life'; 'Why should I love the stepchildren as much as my own children?' These, and many more opinions concerning their children, are openly voiced by mothers and fathers in stepfamilies, just as they are within first-time families.

If you are embarking on a new relationship in which children are involved, or if you are already deeply committed within a stepfamily, I hope that you will be encouraged, as I was, by the many stories that have genuinely happy outcomes. My wish is that you will find your family blending happily together as the years go by, and that you will, given time, enjoy making friends with your stepchildren and receive all the genuine friendship you deserve in return. May it become a story of real success.

R.W.

1
Shall We Get Together?

Expectations

Expectations sound exciting, but they have to be realistic when contemplating the creation of a stepfamily. You have to have faith in yourself as well as in your partner – togetherness is going to be all important. Obviously, all this could be said before embarking on any marriage, but when there are children involved it is essential that you believe your new relationship is worth all the hard work that will be needed to make it successful – and to make it last.

There are countless stories – constantly highlighted by the media – of single mothers, broken homes, absent parents, and child abuse within stepfamilies. The successful stories with happy endings seldom make the headlines.

Stepfamily myths

Two opposing myths have surrounded stepfamilies for many generations – the first being *idealism*: 'We love each other, so this time around we'll all be happy.' When one or both partners have suffered unhappy first marriages, they dream that this time they will make it work. Sometimes the children will pick up on this dream and fantasize about a new parent who will love them more than the one who deserted them. An only child may look forward to living within a larger family. And those partners who have no children of their own often believe they will immediately be accepted as an instant father or mother. Where one parent has died, that family remembers happy times together, and may assume that family life is always wonderful.

It is essential never to rush into the relationship – the failure rate for second and subsequent marriages is higher than that for first-time marriages. Imagine a child's feelings when a family breaks up for a second, or even a third, time:

Rose was not quite two years old when her parents split up. At first she lived with her mother, then when her father, Paul, found a new partner – Jane – she spent the week with them and the weekends with her mother. As she grew older she began to call her stepmother 'Mummy Jane' and came to love both the mothers in her young life. Her birth mother could never quite come to grips with the situation, but Jane had grown to love Paul's child. She found it very hard when Rose sometimes blurted out, 'You are not my real mum!'

'I never wanted a child of my own,' said Jane, 'as I thought it would be too traumatic for Rose. After all, she had three different adults disciplining her. Paul and I, and Rose's mother, would have three-way meetings, looking at our boundaries. For example, Rose would sleep in her mother's bed, and then expect to sleep in mine (with Paul), and it was too hard to explain the difference to a small child. I joined a Parent Group to ask if I was coping well enough. I learned there how difficult stepparenting can be.'

Then, when Rose was seven, her father split up with Jane and found yet another partner. His young daughter was confused and saddened to lose 'Mummy Jane', and Jane was upset at losing this child that she had virtually been bringing up for five years and had come to love almost as her own. She explained to Rose that although she was not living with her daddy any more, she still loved her and would continue to visit her. 'I still check up on her, but have gradually faded out of her life. But I miss her and still love her. If Rose wants to see me again in the future, that's fine – but I think it's kinder to stay away now, or she will get really confused. I found the hardest thing was leaving. I would never jump into such a situation again!'

Before attempting to create a stepfamily, both partners have to believe that getting together could enhance their lives, without wrecking those of the children involved. This will mean including the children's birth parents in future plans, and may well entail learning many new practical parenting skills. In other words, as in any long-term relationship, partners have to work at it and not expect instant success, for otherwise they are bound to be disappointed. Too often I've heard stepparents sigh, 'If only I'd known what I was in for!'

For stepmothers such as Janet, however, there were never any doubts. She had married a widower with three young daughters. She had known their mother – in fact, she had been a nanny to the children before and after their mother died. Janet loved them, and they all loved her. When their father proposed marriage, it seemed nothing could go wrong.

For the next ten years, all was well – the little girls came to love her as a mother, although she insisted that they call her Janet. She kept the memory of their own mother alive by not changing everything in their home and showing them lots of photographs; she devoted all her time to her husband's family.

One month after they had celebrated their tenth wedding anniversary, when the girls were all in their teens, their father told them that he was going to live with another woman.

'We want to stay with Janet,' they chorused.

'Don't be silly, she's not your mother!' was his callous reply, and he took them all off to another part of the country. As their father, he had the right to do this, and although they are now almost old enough to visit Janet on their own, and will perhaps even choose to live with her in the future, it is not surprising that she too is thinking, 'What did I get myself into?'

Stepmothers

The second myth is that of the *'wicked stepmother'*. The phrase is stuck in the minds of many children who may unconsciously dread living with a strange 'mother'. Mothers have the phrase at the back of their minds too, which makes them tense and over-anxious to please, emphasizing the feelings of unreality in the new family situation.

Sadly, some such stepmothers do still exist. Sally said:

My stepmum was a very cold person. She never mentioned my own mum to me. She always refused to help me, while making a great fuss of her own children. My little sister was only four when our parents split up, and I had to try to be a mother to her. My stepsister was even harder than her mum – she obviously set out to be unkind to us. But if we ever dared talk back to our stepmum, she would tell our dad and he would give her a hug. It was hard for us to witness this.

SHALL WE GET TOGETHER?

Margaret's mother died when she was a baby. Her young father handed her over to a series of aunts and housekeepers, 'so I didn't learn much about mother love'. Then when Margaret was nine years old her father married Doreen, who was very young. From that day on, Margaret's natural mother was not allowed to be mentioned: 'She stole my mum from me. I think she was jealous, she adored my father and I was obviously in the way. She wasn't actually unkind, or hurt me, but she never mothered me. Once we had a young helper in the house and she and I became close – that was the nearest I ever came to being really lovingly cared for.' At one time, an aunt wanted to adopt Margaret, but her father said no. 'I knew then that he loved me and took great care of me, but that he never really gave a thought to my feelings.'

Such unloving, unfeeling, stepmothers don't realize that the harm they do to a child is never forgotten: 'She never came to any of my school concerts or parent days,' said Margaret. Even when she had a tragic car accident as a young adult, her stepmother refused to let her father visit her. 'I didn't think your father needed to go to you,' was her amazing explanation.

Today, with children and grandchildren of her own, Margaret still feels anger inside her. 'When Doreen finally died, my father put a stone on her grave which read: *Beloved mother of Margaret*. This shocked me, and after my father died I had it removed. I also put up my one and only photograph of my own mother.'

Annie, also a grandmother now, still suffers from her childhood with a 'wicked stepmother': 'To this day she tells lies about me to her neighbours. However much I try to help her in her old age, she is always ungrateful and spiteful.'

Clearly, the 'myth' lives on! Thankfully, there are also endless stories of wonderful stepmothers who are managing to refute the common assumptions about life in a stepfamily. These are the women who have appreciated the role they are undertaking, and have faced the realities of their situation. One stepmother, Tina, expressed this well: 'I knew that because Jim loved me it did not mean that the rest of his family would feel the same way.'

But did Tina also realize that loving Jim did not necessarily mean that she would love his children? It is never reasonable to expect to do so straight away. Some women actively dislike their partner's children. Mandy refused to let her husband's daughter visit him while she was at home! No doubt his daughter was delighted! But what a sad situation. Given time, Mandy might well have come to be very fond of that little girl.

Stepfathers

There is also a fear associated with the word 'stepfather'. Frequently, when a tragic story of child abuse, or even murder, is told in the media, it is the stepfather who is the first suspect. Sadly, this fear is not a myth. Studies by organizations such as Relate show that stepfathers are five times more likely to sexually abuse children than are natural fathers. But for men who genuinely love children, and long for a family, it is not an easy stigma to live with, and may account for the fact that many stepfathers tend to show indifference towards their partner's children.

As for the children, unless they are very young, they will have read and heard about such stepfathers. So, as a mother, you must face their – probably unspoken – fears. You have to talk openly with them, and reassure them of your determination to create a new, happy home. The important thing will be to let them feel secure by knowing that they can always talk to you; always tell you their worries and fears. Even if they will not be living with you all the time, make sure they know you will be ready to listen to them whenever they need you.

The majority of full-time stepparents are fathers, for it is still more usual following divorce for the children to live with their mother. So when she remarries, her children become part of the package. 'I keep my distance on the whole,' says Peter, who has a close relationship with the children's mother, and adds that, 'In spite of all the nasty stories in the tabloids about stepfathers, I don't regret my new role at all, and in fact it has added a new dimension to my life.'

Greg, also a kindly stepfather, says, 'I leave the discipline to the children's mother.' Hopes are always high that the new relationship will work but expectations will vary according to your previous status: married, single (with or without children), divorced, or widowed. The past you bring with you to the new relationship will affect your emotional response to your new family. It is not easy to separate completely from your previous situation – there may be lingering guilt, anger, or sadness; regrets abound. If such problems from a previous marriage have not been sufficiently sorted out, the pressure on the new stepfamily will be very great. Accordingly, some parents feel that by making a 'clean break' they can blot out the past. This is not so simple when there are children around.

Yet some prospective stepparents forget that it is not just their new partner's children who make up the whole 'stepping' package – there is the ex-partner also, who is the children's natural parent (see Chapter 8).

Ex-partners

When Linda met Jack he was newly separated from his first wife, Anita. He was desperately unhappy, for Anita had walked out on him taking their two-year-old son, Sam, with her. Her reason? She found him boring; he seemed to have no interests except his rather dreary job in a paint factory, and she knew that marrying him when she was only 18 had been a dreadful mistake. Anita was lively and outgoing, loved a social life, and adored playing with Sam, while Jack insisted on strict discipline.

Linda knew none of this: 'Jack told me that Anita had run off with another man, and was a lazy wife, a far too casual mother to their son, and that she had broken his heart.' So Linda married Jack and bore him three more children. Sam would visit them regularly and enjoy meeting his half-siblings (he and Anita had moved to another part of the country). It was not until about ten years later that Linda and Jack went on a seaside holiday and found themselves in the same village as Anita. The children were all delighted to be together, and Linda found Anita a loving, caring mother, quite unlike the girl Jack had described to her. Linda said: 'She was a wonderful mother, although sadly her second marriage had left her a widow. She and I talked mostly about the children, and then realized that we had a lot in common. We now exchange letters and even photographs of our families, and Jack is naturally delighted – if somewhat bewildered – by the situation!'

It is not unusual for the ex-wife or husband to be described as unfaithful, as Anita was, or demonized in some other way in order to make the new partner feel special. And it is an equally common situation for the first and second wives to be vilified by each other. The first wife is often dismissed as unloving, and the second as a scheming adulterer.

Mary said:

'I lapped up all my husband said about his first wife, about her affairs and her extravagance, until I met his children – who obviously adored their mother. They made it obvious that they thought I was to blame for their father leaving home. No way were they going to let me forget that.' Mary was shattered by the thought of her new role. 'Even though Dan's children only visited us once a fortnight, I felt I had to go out when they came. I used to cook special meals for them, but they kept saying how they missed their food at home. Their mother would phone up before they arrived and refuse to speak to me, then tell my husband what they were to eat and drink. My fond hopes of being a stepmother all vanished – I felt like a sort of unwanted auntie.'

The shadow of a former partner often hangs over a stepparent in this way. In many cases sympathy for the ex-partner is well deserved, but how hard it is for a new stepparent to appreciate this. Mary took a long time to understand her stepchildren's feelings, and only by never trying to discipline them, or criticize them, or being anything other than friendly towards them, have they finally accepted her as a member of the family. But Mary needed Dan's help too, and this she did not get for a long time. 'He couldn't grasp how I felt – he only said all children were difficult to please and what was I worrying about!'

Becoming a stepparent with no children of your own

This is a new situation for you to face. As well as adjusting to living with a new partner, you are about to become an instant parent!

'I had not even spoken to a child since I had been one myself!' said one young man who fell in love with a widow with four daughters. 'I never gave the girls a thought.' Not until he found himself spreading peanut butter and honey on eight pieces of toast at breakfast, and listening to *Top of the Pops* instead of the evening news, was he forced to give those children a lot more than just a thought.

You may have excited feelings, such as Patricia, who said: 'Imagine having a little girl. Even though she's not my own daughter, I know we'll be great friends.' Patricia's mother, however, warned her daughter about taking on a stepchild. 'How will you cope, dear, with another man's child? If he divorced the child's mother, you must surely be worried?' Patricia, though, was scornful of her mother's doubts: 'I know what I'm doing.' However, her expectations were soon dashed when the little girl greeted her with 'I hate you, you stole my dad!'

Graham's expectations were also bordering on the optimistic when he was faced with a trio of schoolboys as his stepchildren: 'I always wanted to be part of a family, and here's a ready-made one. It'll be great.' It took Graham some time before a true sense of realism hit home, and he learned to tread warily, have patience, and show the children how much he cared about them without trying to become a surrogate dad: 'Eventually I became a sort of family friend, rather like an uncle – it worked well.'

Nigel had no children of his own when he met and fell in love with Kate:

'She was so loving and caring, how could her three kids not be the same? I knew that their dad had walked out on them, so I guessed they must hate him and would therefore love me. How wrong could I be? They think their dad is wonderful, and keep talking about him. Kate finds this quite natural, and sometimes I feel like a sort of outsider – you know, four against one.'

Nigel says he is 'hanging in there', but his expectations of becoming an instant father have been shattered. He has accepted the role of 'Mum's friend' and now, after two years, all three children have admitted that 'he's OK to have around'. That sounds to me as if he's made it!

Conversely, Charles, who had suffered as a schoolboy when his own parents split up, said:

'My dad had several relationships, and he always had more to do with his partner's children than with me and my brothers. We grew up in a family where we didn't talk to each other, but when mum and dad first parted, both of them felt the need to explain things to me. It would have felt disloyal to talk to anyone else about it, and so I kept it to myself. It lowered my expectations of what I might receive from my own stepchildren.'

Charles had counselling for several years when he first left home, but his childhood memories made him very cautious when he began a relationship with a divorcee who had two children.

Peter, who had been in a childless marriage, began a new partnership with a single mum who had two young teenagers:

When we first got together I never thought about her family, until one day she said, 'What about my children?' She had every confidence that all would be well, and I believed her. So it was all somewhat of a shock, and for a while life was not easy. The children and I had some battles royal! The thing is, I still believe in teaching kids the value of everything, and that you have to work for things. But their mum says I'm living in the fifties! Of course she and the kids are three people who form a unit, from which I am excluded. Like so many girls with their stepfathers, Sian tends to say, 'You're not my dad, so why should I do what you say?' And I once chucked the boy out of the house – but of course I went after him – although I guess that could happen if he were my own teenage son. Mostly, though, I don't talk to them directly on matters of discipline, but through their mother. You know, 'Tell them to do this or that!' I have just had to accept that the children come before me, and of course I never look on them as my own. However, my partner and I have a very strong relationship, and that's what makes it all happen, all work. I would do it all again.'

Becoming a stepparent when you both have children

The organization Relate likes to talk of 'blending', rather than 'stepping', families. But whatever you call two families starting to live together in one home, it can still be a traumatic event. Two households, neither one wanting to change their ways of living, will take a long time to settle down. Family therapists say it can take up to three years for a stepfamily to be thoroughly integrated.

Ann and Eliza were school friends, often spending a few days at a time in each other's houses. Then Ann's mother told her daughter that she was going to move in with Eliza's father. 'You love staying with her, don't you, dear?' At first Ann agreed, but it was different now. This wasn't home. This wasn't her daddy coming in every night. And Eliza hated Ann's mother living in her house, cooking in her mummy's kitchen.

In spite of being an experienced mum to five children, even Emma had rather too many unrealistic expectations when she became a stepmother to two more: 'I soon came to understand that it is important to think about ritual – to be sure that no one is left out. We all moved into Paul's house and his elder daughter was quite put out – she had been playing mum!' There were also emotions she had not anticipated: 'I felt jealousy. I had not expected this, but I found I was very jealous indeed of the time that Paul gave to his girls.'

Sally, on the other hand, was only 20 when she met her husband, who had two sons aged four and seven: 'I had no idea how to behave with children, and thought it best just to treat them as people. And I suppose because I was so young I could be quite dispassionate, and so they talked to me quite openly. What I had not anticipated was that their own mother would resent me and made the children feel the same. Only when I had children of my own did I understand how she must have felt.'

Within many stepfamilies, the children themselves will be filled with jealousies and harsh criticisms will be flung around. It is possibly wise for each birth parent to continue disciplining their own youngsters, but take care – the stepchildren may feel you don't care about them. This is when your relationship with your partner must be at its strongest. Agreeing on discipline, on household rules (written or unwritten) that both families can understand, is essential (see Chapter 6).

Of course, for many children today, family life already involves many changes – nothing seems permanent. So before the two families are finally brought together, this is one of the many things you have to talk about instead of creating idealistic expectations. Is your love strong enough to survive all the problems that will arise –

SHALL WE GET TOGETHER?

financial, social, and domestic? Are you ready for the doubts and confusion that will emerge as your children face their new future – probably against their wishes? Are you ready to tell them what that future will hold?

2
Consulting the Children

Divorce usually takes place during the first ten years of a marriage, and therefore the children will still be quite young. Of those who divorce, over 60 per cent remarry, and around one-sixth of second marriages also break down. Many children are constantly in a state of transition – their lives rarely free from disruption and acrimony. When considering taking a child into a new family, the past family life must not be forgotten. One child may have lived with a single parent for some years, one may have come from foster care, another may have experienced the death of a parent, or already have one stepparent. All will have suffered significant losses – how much more trauma can they cope with? I remember one little girl crying at the news that her mother was to remarry. It turned out that the child's main worry was that, having divorced one man, her mother would divorce another. 'Will you still love me, Mum?' was her unspoken question.

It is vital to prepare the children for yet another change in their lives. Enormous understanding, as well as masses of reassurance that they are still loved, is going to be needed when telling them that their parent is taking on a new partner. They will need to understand what role the parent who is not coming with them is going to play in their future, what role a new stepparent is going to take, and that all the adults in their lives still care about them. And if each of their parents has found a new partner, there will suddenly be *four* significant adults in their lives – albeit that two of them will only be part-time parents. This will take a great deal of careful explanation. Comments such as 'Why doesn't Dad love us any more?' will not be easy to answer. What all children want is to be loved – and more especially to be understood. They must be given time to consider all the implications of this news – loyalty to their other parent, where they will live, how much the new partner will figure in their lives. Foremost in most children's minds will be the thought of how they can stay in touch with the parent who has left home: 'I only see Dad every two weeks anyway, will I still be able to do that?' Children almost always have great sympathy for the parent who is not remarrying, and feel protective towards them, which can cause huge resentment towards the stepparent. Far too often I have heard children say that they were not told enough: 'We were not talked *with*, only talked *to*.' As when discussing divorce or bereavement, information is seldom fully explained, and certainly never repeated.

The need for communication

Child psychiatrists stress that communication in stepfamilies, and how the complexities have been discussed and explained, continues to be of importance to children who need to process information by repeating conversations over time, not through a single 'telling'. Often, a child will shy away from a conversation, perhaps try to change the subject, but inside he will have a strong need to talk over the past, and to be reassured about the future. In particular, he must know that none of the problems are his fault, for such losses can cause a child to feel inadequate and blame himself. Remember this is a situation over which he has no control. And you will find, as children grow older, that some of the information you originally gave them will need to be updated. Children need to know that they can ask questions, and receive honest answers. Too often they are lied to – possibly when a parent is trying, mistakenly, to save them from hurt.

'Why did nobody tell us anything?'

'We knew Mum and Dad quarrelled a lot, but they kept telling us they had a secret – nothing to do with us. I loved secrets, but I came to hate that one – it seemed more like a conspiracy after a while.'

Depending on their ages, children want to know if they will have to move house, or school, or share a bedroom, or leave a beloved dog behind. Tough as such information may be, for emotions will be strong at this time, it is better to be honest in what you tell children, rather than let them find out later. They will not readily forgive you for keeping them 'in the dark'. Younger children have been known to ask, 'If Dad gets married, will you still be my mum?' Such questions sometimes lead parents to decide to cohabit rather than marry – hoping that that will make the children feel more secure.

Children need to know:

- What role the new parent is going to take.
- That the parent's new marriage does not mean they won't be loved any more.
- The full picture of what is happening – the arrangements that are being made.
- Details of any extended family involved – step-siblings, possible step-grandparents, etc.

Meeting the stepchildren

And what about that significant first meeting with a future stepchild? This can be of great concern for timing is all important, and you hope that the child has been spoken to beforehand. If you have children of your own, it is a good idea to include them in your first date, providing that you have already told them about your new friend. If you can show interest in the children, without bombarding them with too many questions, this could lead to further, less formal, meetings. Ideally, for younger children, the outing could be a casual one – perhaps a picnic, or a visit to the zoo.

> James had been married before, but had no children, when he met a widow with two daughters. She told him at once about the girls, and brought them with her when they first met: 'We went to a National Trust garden and we hit it off, gelled as a family. Within three months we decided to live together, and I moved into her home.' His eldest stepdaughter, now a school-leaver, told me that she remembers her mother choosing James: 'And we liked him. She had always told us if and when she chose a man she would tell him that we all came as a package! We did not take James's surname; we all agreed it was important for us to have our real dad as a role model. We have created our own family, better than many real families.'

> Betsy did not introduce Philip to her children straight away: 'I wanted to be sure he was Mr Right! There was absolutely no way I could have stayed with him if he had not been nice to the children. After all, a large part of me had been created by being a mother. I waited nearly six months, and even then I only told the

children he was a special friend and not that we were thinking of living together. This was because my own mother had remarried without telling me when I was only about ten years old. I never wanted to inflict such a shock on my own girls.'

Bill, separated father of eight-year-old Gary, had not intended to give his young son a shock – but he certainly gave him a surprise. Being a very reserved person, Bill kept putting off telling Gary that he was intending to marry his friend Barbara. Then one day when the three of them were having lunch together, the vicar walked in and started talking about dates for the wedding! It was not the way Bill had meant the boy to find out. Barbara tried to soften the blow by telling Gary about the new house they were moving into, showed him his new room, and told him he could arrange it how he liked – but the boy seemed uninterested: 'Perhaps he was jealous, and I'm sure he realized he would be transient in our home.'

David's stepchildren were also never told directly about their mother's new relationship, but because they were introduced casually over a period of time they accepted him almost without question: 'We all met initially at a party and Polly told me that she was divorced. The children always came with her when we met and seemed to get used to me being around. Even one time when I had supper in their house and they saw I was still around the next morning, they seemed to take it quite casually. Throughout that summer we spent a lot of time together and a year later I moved into Polly's home permanently. Perhaps because the children went to their natural father for the weekends, there was little tension in the house. The elder girl has been receptive towards me from the start, and although the younger one is not often actually rude, she is more reserved, more curious about my relationship with her mother. At times she worries us, has little self-esteem, and tries in small ways to harm herself. I tend to hold back, I don't want to be demanding.'

'I forgot to mention that I have some children!'
If it is vital to tell your children about your new relationship, what about the question of telling your new partner about your children? Laura said:

'My partner did not tell me straight off that he had children! I had known him for some time when we were in the local park one day and I reached into his briefcase for a pen and found a pair of children's knickers! He told me he kept them for his youngest daughter in case she needed to change when he picked her up from nursery school.' Laura said her partner had felt no need to tell her as the children lived with their mum. 'I forgave him as we were such good friends by then; the little girls were used to a fairly social life with their mum, so eventually when I met them they accepted me quite happily. When I began living with their dad, they would visit us every other weekend, and one of them seemed genuinely pleased that I was making her dad happy. The other girl has periods of resentment, and certainly knows how to put me down from time to time! I know it would be worse if they were with us all the time. But it would not have put me off getting together with their dad.'

Daphne never knew that her husband had any children until they had been married for nearly three years! She was still in her early twenties, and her husband, who came from another country, was older than her. When he suggested they visit his old home, she was excited, and when they arrived his family all rushed out to welcome her. But when two young women came out and cried out 'Daddy!' to her husband, Daphne was struck dumb. But worse was to come – one of these two young women had a baby daughter of her own. Daphne had become a stepmother and step-grandmother all at once. They all loved her, tried to make her happy, but not surprisingly Daphne's marriage did not last.

Jenny was only 23 when she began living with her partner, Tim: 'I had never been a baby sort of person – my sister had a baby, but I was not an enthusiastic aunt. When I found out that Tim had a daughter, Natasha, aged five, it had a strange effect on the way I behaved; I was concerned how I looked, would she compare me with her mother? I had met her mother, but at the time I never thought about her point of view – she must have hated me. That first time I met Natasha, Tim went round to fetch her at teatime. I prepared an enormous spread as Tim had said she liked a lot to eat! It was all very formal; I realize now that I showed Natasha no warmth – I was just hurt when she said she didn't want anything to eat. Her dad was quite cross with her, and sat her on his knee.

'Now, it all makes me cringe when I think how young she was, and how odd she must have been feeling. I had no idea how to behave with young children, was the youngest in my own family, and just had no natural mothering instincts. However, it became a regular arrangement. Every Friday after school Tim would fetch Natasha and on Sunday nights I would take her home. She was a quiet child, and would sit under the table when we had our friends round. I never thought to find her any toys.

'Subsequently, I have since felt guilty, but somehow Natasha took it all in her stride. In fact, she wanted the three adults in her life to be friends. "Why can't you two live with Mum, then we can all be together?" she would say. She even suggested that we move in with her mum, "so that Dad and Mum can share the double bed and you and I can sleep in the bunk beds in my room"! After this I realized how children must be told that it is possible to love, or at least like, several adults at one time – and with Natasha we had to make her understand that I was here in her life and her dad's life for good, and that her parents would never be getting back together.'

'Are all children allowed to have their say?'

Things were very different for one young brother and sister. Their father had walked out when they were only about six and three. Their mother met the man who would be their stepfather several years later, and only began to live with him when the children were in their teens:

> When we first lived together, I asked the children about remarrying and they both said 'no way', very firmly. Then after another few years, they said definitely yes! I would never have married while they were still so young, and certainly not until they agreed to it. I've always put them first – I protect them. When my husband criticizes their behaviour, I take it as a personal insult to me and the way I bring them up – it hurts me. Happily they like my new husband, and eventually chose to change their name to his. They refer to us together as Mum and Dad, but never call him 'Dad' to his face, although they give him

Father's Day cards. They played a vital part in my decision to marry.

Children understand feelings far more than we give them credit for:

> Sarah was only ten when she and her seven-year old brother were taken to live with their mother's new partner, Richard. Sarah had met Richard some months before, and her mother (Verity) had told her several weeks ahead what was happening and that they would be moving. Verity thought her daughter understood all the arrangements, but Sarah's main worries were: 'Did Richard really want us living with him? Then I worried about my dad left all alone. We visited him on Sundays and I worried that he was not managing well, so I would try to clean his kitchen and check that the milk was not sour in the fridge!'
>
> Sarah's young brother, only seven at the time, was not quite so ready to accept his new home. As Sarah explained, 'We never quite knew how my brother felt, although he was obviously upset inside. He would creep along the corridor into Mum's and Richard's room, and leap into bed in the morning beside my mum! But he did not dislike Richard, and they get on well now.'
>
> It seems that many of Verity's and Richard's worries over Sarah and her brother were not the same as those of the children's – and this is not unusual. Sarah again: 'Dad was great, he never foul-mouthed my mum, though once or twice he asked me, "Do you think she will come back?" I was sad then because I knew she would not; she and Richard were so obviously happy together. Mum and Richard married when I was 16, and I went to their wedding.'
>
> Sarah was not quite so easy-going, though, when her own dad decided to settle down again: 'When I was about 13 or 14, Carol moved in with Dad. I was not at all nice to her! Then one day I found a note on my bed from Carol saying, "You are always welcome to come and stay" and that made me like her better. I went to their wedding too. And when she had her first baby my brother and I were both pleased. Dad had taken us out to lunch to tell us, thinking we might be upset, but we were delighted! Mum and Richard also discussed babies, but decided to get a dog instead!

> 'Richard has a daughter too, but her mother always told her lies about my family. I was lucky, I was always told the truth, always put in the picture. Dad always considered my feelings. I remember once he actually asked me, "Would you mind if Carol stayed the night?" I was embarrassed, and wished they would just get on with it! But in fact I would have been hurt if they had not told me, and I was grateful to Dad for his consideration.'

Some young parents, especially single mothers or divorced fathers, are often reluctant to reveal the fact that they have a child, or several children, when they start a new relationship. 'I thought it might put her off' is a usual explanation for the secrecy. One young mother was heard to say, 'I love my two babies, but I can't expect any man to love me when he hears about them.'

Such young people are understandably anxious about telling a new friend that they are not totally unattached. Whether a young man has his children living with him on a full or part-time basis, he knows that he will never be completely free to build up a relationship on a one-to-one basis. A single mum will always have to find a baby-sitter before accepting a date; to feed her family rather than prepare a candlelit dinner for two. Practical problems will always come between a couple when there are children involved. Many people find it hard to establish a strong relationship when their partner's family is around. They never get the time to develop a joint lifestyle for themselves – the partner with the ready-made family will have an ongoing situation which may be difficult for the other partner to fit into. 'How on earth could we ever have a honeymoon with twin toddlers?' said Judy, almost on the verge of tears. 'I love Ted so much, but he seems to think we can go to a luxury hotel for a week and that they'll play happily in the next room!'

The birth parent must not be forgotten

It is easy when talking with such families to forget the feelings of the birth parent:

> When Maggie and her husband, both in their forties, divorced, they made amicable arrangements for the children – they would live mainly with their mother, but they had a strict rota for visiting their father: once a week during term time and two full

weeks during the holidays. Maggie says: 'They loved their time with their father, and I never begrudged it – but now that he has a girlfriend, and she's only about 22, I feel resentment that she will be around when they should be having time with their father on his own. I mean, how can she take care of my children – she has no experience of mothering. I'm so afraid I'm going to lose them – what if she tries to be a sort of stepmother to them?'

George, whose wife took their baby daughter to Australia when they separated over eight years ago, still finds such a loss hard to bear: 'Her mother does bring the child over, and she spends many holidays with me, but the emotional break took a long while for me, it was so painful. What I find hardest is seeing her off at the airport each time. We both get depressed for a few days beforehand and there are always tearful goodbyes. It makes me more and more aware of the split. But I phone her every week and send her copies of her favourite magazine too.

'I was introduced to her stepfather soon after he married my ex-wife, and it was a friendly meeting. My daughter was school age by then and we told her she could listen to our discussions about her future – schooling, etc. She knows she is welcome to walk in at any time, or open a door and listen. But I am conscious my daughter is wondering if my feelings will be hurt if she shows affection for her stepfather. She is obviously shy of showing affection to him in my presence, though not the other way round – she never hides her love towards me.'

George is one birth parent who has managed to face reality and look at the positive points before the negative ones. He once said, 'If you are too possessive, you will lose that child in the end. It is all about trying to see more love in the new situation as an asset, rather than a problem. Yes, be defensive and cautious, a relative newcomer's influence over one's child is hard to face, but you are given no choice! So, at first, give them the benefit of the doubt.'

George is perhaps more fortunate than many fathers who – in spite of supposedly sharing parental responsibilities – are prevented from seeing their children by their ex-wives. The mothers whisk the children away, telling the younger ones that their father doesn't want to see them any more. Some are even accused, falsely, of abusing their own children.

CONSULTING THE CHILDREN

When starting a relationship with a man or woman who has children – either living with them or not – it is essential to consider the other birth parent. However harsh a picture your new partner may paint of an ex-husband or ex-wife, you can never deny their existence, and it would be foolish to ignore their feelings. Many stepparents tell me that once they have children of their own they are more able to do this: 'Now I know the sort of permanent feelings it arouses, the strong, almost fierce, emotions that bind you to that child for life.' Shirley was speaking for many first-time parents – mothers and fathers – when she added her own baby to a family of stepchildren.

It is usually the children who have the greater reservations about creating a new family. Many of them cling to the hope that their parents will get back together, however unreasonable this may seem, and however much they may like, or respect, their parent's new partner. (Remember little Natasha suggesting that her stepmother come to live with her mother!) However, once a half-brother or half-sister arrives, any hopes of their own parents living together again are dashed.

In almost every situation, it is wiser to tell the whole family what is happening. Not being honest with them, locking up your emotions, and keeping children guessing (and their fantasies are often far more frightening than the truth), will never help to solve a crisis.

3
Endless Complexities

Few children today are being brought up in what is called a nuclear family – the stereotypical two adults and 2.4 children. There are extended families; teenage families; one-parent families; families where both adults are female – or both male; there are stepfamilies; and countless other even more complex situations. None of these types necessarily involves a legal marriage (see Chapter 9).

Within each type of family, further alternative arrangements occur. Within stepfamilies, as well as other types of family, there are endless variations. Some of these are listed below.

Setting up home with a partner who has children living away from home

This scenario is usually one where the birth father and his new partner are living together, while his children are living with his ex-partner:

> When I married Bill he was divorced with a ten-year-old son, Gary, who was living with his mother. I had hesitated about the marriage – I knew there could be strained relationships within stepfamilies. And Gary has not been too easy. He is a quiet, rather anti-social child. He behaves in a rather sullen manner, and often ignores me. Sometimes he will ring up, and if I answer the phone he won't talk at all – which is awkward if I'm alone. Yet when he is with us, usually for his half-terms or long weekends, he wants to know exactly what we have been doing. If he sees photos of us on holiday, he asks why he was not with us! When we had to live in London because of Bill's work, Gary became more distant towards me, and wanted more and more of a share of his father. Of course he blames me for the fact that he sees less of his dad now we have moved south. I would not recommend marrying anyone with children, though as Gary is seldom with us now, it is not really difficult. Sometimes we take him on outings with us and it seems to work.

Laura, who only found out that her future partner had two children by chance (remember how she found the little girl's knickers in his briefcase!), has no such strong feelings:

> I only see the children occasionally now and I suppose that means I have the best of both worlds really – I like being with them and miss them more than I thought I would. I opt out of doing too much parenting! And I feel sure their mum would back me up when I reprimand them – which I have to at times – certainly the eldest one. She can be infuriating (like all teenagers), and she was continually rude to me when we were on holiday and I got upset. She did apologize later, saying she had been the same with her mum's second husband as well. I think she is really trying to get along with me now.

Jenny, who became a stepmother while still very young and was upset in later years to think how ignorant of childcare she was, has wise advice to anyone contemplating sharing their home with a partner's child. 'Of course,' she says, 'the relationship between the two adults must be strong. And you must be aware that you are always going to have to share your life with the children. Yes, I would warn anyone of these things, but would never put them off.'

Carol puts the success of her stepfamily down to the fact that she never tried to be a stepmother, and never uses the term if she can avoid it: 'I refer to the children as "Alistair's children". When we first got together, and Alistair visited their mother, I did not go with him every time. And I would discuss such things as pop groups or clothes with Alistair's daughter, instead of asking rather motherly questions! This seemed to work, and we are now good friends.'

Malcolm was devastated when his wife ran off with their two-year-old son, with the results that he had to have counselling for several years. Happily for him, he found a new partner, Amy, who was only too happy to welcome the boy into their home. They set up a strict rota for the child to visit them on alternate weekends. At first, the little boy accepted Amy, who made him nice meals and read him bedtime stories. However, as he grew older, Amy felt great tension when he visited them. 'The trouble was with my ex-wife,' said Malcolm. 'Sadly, she is unstable and upsets Amy with abusive phone calls, so my son never feels at ease. It is so sad, for the boy is an outgoing child; he knows he can trust Amy after all these years, yet he is alienating her so much that she is often reduced to tears during his visits. She simply does not know how to behave towards him any more. He once asked her what he should call her, and she wisely suggested he call her his friend – and I try to show him what a kind person she is. But then my ex-wife phones yet again to complain, and the tension starts to build up.'

When James first met his present wife, she was a widow with two daughters. Right from the start, they both wanted the new relationship to work: 'And it was easier than I thought,' said James. 'Of course the girls were jealous; they had had their mum to themselves for nearly ten years. At first I moved into their home, but after six months we decided to move to my house which meant the girls moving school. Life was full of tensions then because of the newness of everything, but once they settled down it was all right. They both had only dim memories of their dad. A big issue when I first came along had been that the eldest girl had acted as a sort of surrogate father (her mother admitted this) and had looked after her baby sister. However, now she could relax and be a child again. On a few issues of behaviour I felt I should lay down the law, and smacked them once or twice! Their mother said 'How dare you?' and such times caused stress, but we nearly always presented a united front. We spent family holidays together, all deciding where to go and what to do – it was a novelty for me. And we all talked a lot. We had arguments right out in the open.

'I would suggest parents have a sort of trial run at joining another family if possible – as we did. It is a tremendous personal effort to put the others first. In the beginning the children seemed self-centred to me, and I questioned why I should help them. But soon I experienced great joy when they both treated me as a father. Yes, it took a massive amount of effort – it can seem as if you're losing at the first sign of tension. Who would believe you would *want* to smack them – but your patience goes! I suppose if you can't accept change, children are not for you. Your very being is challenged on a daily basis. If you are not willing to grow and compromise with young growing people around you, you had better bail out! As for me – I sometimes think being a stepfather is better than the real thing! There's no duty involved, and it comes naturally, providing you give them freedom of self-expression.'

Setting up home when one partner's children live with you and the other partner's children live elsewhere

When Helen first met Hugh her daughter was two and Hugh's girls, seven and nine, lived with their mother. 'They only joined us every other weekend, and at first I tried mothering them, but perhaps I put too much effort into it. One or other would say to me, "You're not my mum, you can't tell me off." So I would answer that when they were in my house they had to do what I wanted. Hugh always backed me up on this. There was a certain amount of jealousy around – I remember feeling that my husband devoted too much time to his children. In the early days he would take the children home, bath them, put them to bed, and perhaps stay and have a drink with his ex-wife – all very amicable. But somehow this led the girls into a false sense of security, and they kept asking, "Why don't you still live together?" So now he finds it better simply to drop them off and say, "Love you, goodbye." Also, as she grew older, there were a few clashes between my daughter and my husband – they play one off against the other. I tend to tell him he didn't do that with his two!

'My husband and I are very close. It is now quite hard for his two daughters as their mother is having another baby. I try to help them, but there is no natural bonding between us; you have to work hard at your affection for stepchildren. Sometimes they still cause problems between me and Hugh, because I find it hard not to step in. I then hear the children saying, "They are having a row about me!" When I overstep the mark, or Hugh does, it feels worse. I do try to treat them all equally, and I had a good childhood myself. Now I try to keep things in the family running smoothly. I have a special rapport with my eldest stepdaughter, who did not get on with her own mother. The younger girl still sticks to Hugh; she adores him. I try not to be the wicked stepmother!

'If they lived with us all the time I think I would behave differently. As it is, they treat our house like a hotel and never tidy their rooms – though they are getting better! One of them still accuses me of hating her own mother (which I do!), but I tell her she will understand when she is older. If I didn't have children or if Hugh didn't, I think it would be harder. But Hugh and I are in the same situation, which pleased us both when we met. Of course, jealousy must have set in a little when I kept my daughter all the time and Hugh only had his girls every other weekend – it must have hurt him, been in the back of his mind.

'When reality kicks in, you realize you don't love his kids as much as your own – you can't! Everyone feels the same if they are honest; it is difficult. And of course for the children to be thrown into a family that is not their own is very hard. Children are not stupid, but they come to respect your love for their parent. Some parents run their stepchildren down all the time – a part of me understands that – but luckily Hugh always backs me up when I say his girls are a nightmare: he understands. We all know that stepchildren test you out, see how far they can go – just like your own kids do! I sometimes say to the three girls, Hugh's two and my one, "You are lucky, you have two homes, two families." I think it is unique if you achieve a really close relationship with a stepchild. If you foster or adopt them that is your choice, but with stepchildren you have them thrust upon you – they come as part of the deal with your partner.'

Celia had two boys of nine and eleven, and a daughter of seven, when she met Don, who also had a daughter of seven, and two slightly younger sons, eight and nine. Both were still married and subsequently admitted to having acrimonious divorces. Celia had enough money from her marriage settlement to buy a new house for her and her three children, and – at her youngest child's request – asked Don to join her. This he did, leaving his three children with their mother. However, they visited their father every other weekend, while Celia's children only spent Sunday afternoons with their dad. 'I didn't really know what I was getting myself into,' says Celia. 'But I was determined to make it work. I even tried to get them all together for a family meal, thinking it would work, but it was a disaster, they all hated it! I was not always in agreement with Don. I was rather like a mother hen and hated it if he criticized my children. But we do talk things over, which is good. One of the problems was that my eldest son was very confident, and my stepson was not, so I made a fuss of the stepchild with the result that my own child lost (or pretended to lose) his own confidence. Then my stepdaughter became very jealous of my daughter; they were both the same age and at the same school, but she had been the baby of her family, with two older brothers, and was now being very difficult.

'The children are all very different. The boys used to hit each other, but were never too bad to us. My eldest son took himself off in his teens and had counselling, possibly because one stepbrother was one of those who always did well at school, and was very popular. When he was 14, the eldest boy was caught shoplifting, and was in trouble with the police at times, though not seriously. But the girls were never like that. They had a good bond between them. Mind you, they have always been more emotional – especially during their teens. My stepdaughter ran out of the house one evening and we had to chase after her.

'I would never put anyone off being a stepparent. It is hard, but I don't regret a minute of it. I feel an affinity with others in the same position. You know, my GP once said to me: "You have no history – you need to start making a bit of history together." That was one gift of a saying, because it is so true. The children all have their own histories, and when you marry late you have none – none together, that is. So you have to create some.'

For a stepparent, past experiences of the family a man is marrying into can often accentuate the initial feelings of being an outsider. Don says: 'The children were particularly keen on getting out their old photo albums and reminiscing over their early years – I felt very left out, especially as my ex-wife had taken all my photos. Now, ten years on, we all have shared memories.'

Jessica has certainly been creating a history for herself and her husband Robert. Her first husband left her with two children aged six and three. She was coping well when she met Robert, who had a teenage daughter. 'We did not live together for several years, then for five years Robert moved in with me and my children (without his daughter), and then we eventually married when my two were 13 and 16. They see their father fairly regularly, and he spoils them, so Robert is sometimes jealous. His daughter is a difficult girl, rude to me when she comes round, probably jealous. But my children like Robert, and have even changed their name to his. They call him Dad – but not to his face! We've had our problems, yes. Children and money mostly. I once considered leaving Robert after one of our rows, but when I told my children they were devastated. The thing is, you need to have a very strong relationship when you have children, for you simply have to put them first, and make that very plain to your partner. No, it's not easy, anyone I have spoken to says the same. But then, is marriage easy all the time? Is it easy bringing up children all the time? No!'

Clearly, there are advantages and disadvantages to both of the scenarios listed above: full-time and part-time stepparenting. If it is full time it can be overwhelming, especially when one of you is unused to youngsters in the house. However, part-time stepparents often say that their situation causes even more disruption within the family. Weekends can become filled with complicated visiting arrangements instead of times to relax. But what if all the children move in together? Does that solve all the problems?

Two families living in one household

When Emma remarried five years ago she had five children and her new husband, Alan, had two. 'Yes, we had seven teenagers between us, all living at home! Being used to five, I did not hesitate, and as our two youngest girls were friends already, I thought it would be easy. I now know that it takes time to get close to other people's children. I knew it was important to think about ritual, and be sure that no one was left out.

'We moved into Alan's house, and his eldest was quite put out as she had been playing mum. The most surprising emotion I felt was jealousy – I had not expected this. But I found I was jealous of the time Alan gave to his girls. My parents were helpful, and as a teacher I was used to problems arising. My middle son was difficult, especially with Alan. He got in trouble with the police at one time, and his own dad was of no help.

'And Alan's eldest daughter was a problem too, a difficult girl, probably jealous. She kept hurting herself, cutting her arms and so on. She could be dispassionate, seemingly not feeling any guilt. Sometimes her own mother would turn up and she and her sister would then shout out that I was not their mum. They would say to my daughters, "You have your own mum living here, it's different for you." And of course they are good at manipulating their dad. Mind you, I love them both now; it is hard not to when you are helping to bring them up.'

Rebecca is another mother who took on stepchildren in addition to her own: 'I was 39, divorced, and with a daughter of fourteen and son of thirteen when I inherited three stepchildren. They were the two girls and one little boy of my partner, Ellis, who was divorced from his rather hopeless, uneducated (his words) wife. The children spent nearly all their time with us. I tried to treat the stepchildren in the same way as I treated my own. I worked very hard at it. I think now that this was a mistake. We sure made rocky progress for a while. The eldest stepchild was no problem, but the younger girl was very close to her mother and kept bringing me messages from her – horrid ones. And sometimes when Ellis forgot to take his children round to her mother, or was late, their mum would blame me! I felt jealous at times, for when the children were talking to their father I would cease to exist. Then my children would say to their step-siblings, "We're living with your Dad." You can imagine how they shouted back! For myself, I learned not to push the children too far – they are all so different. I also know now that you must never put kids in the middle of *your* arguments.'

Rebecca wishes now that she had known how all the children were feeling at the time they all moved in together. 'It is hard to understand their emotions when you are so full of mixed feelings of your own. And of course when you inherit stepchildren you don't start from the beginning, do you? You only begin when they have reached certain ages. I was very conscious of the fact that I had not raised my husband's children, knew little of their early years. After all, the first seven years of a child's life are said to be the formative ones, so perhaps I should not have expected to become as close to them as I wanted.'

When living arrangements are not as originally planned

Your plans are well organized; you know whose children will be living with which parent; the future family life is all set to start. Then one day those plans are changed, often with little warning:

Pippa was divorced with three children when she met Ray, who had a young daughter. 'He told me that his little girl was mentally handicapped, but would live with her mother. However, every other weekend the child would be brought to us, which caused quite a lot of stress. My children were older, and were a great help. Then, out of the blue, the girl's mother decided to move overseas and we were landed with the child full time. Not very easy. Put it this way, a two-year-old would have been more alert. She is quite sociable and friendly, but not numerate or literate. She does go to special school, and we are trying, with their help, to teach her independence. Luckily I have a strong relationship with Ray, so we can withstand the stress. But he was never able to talk about the child's problems with his first wife, and so in a way I have had to help him in his attitude towards her.

'Now that my children are married and have their own families, Ray is able, for the first time, to watch a child grow and develop in the normal way – it is an exciting experience for him. We are a happy family – but I never thought when we first married that our future would work out as it has. Even now, Ray is having to be very firm with his first wife and insist she takes some responsibility for their child. We have taken his daughter on holiday with us from time to time, but it is good sometimes to have time to ourselves.'

Fiona also thought that her new family life was settled when she married Tom. She had a seven-year-old daughter and Tom had two children, a girl of nine and a boy of eleven. His children stayed with their mother, so Fiona was still able to have a one-to-one relationship with her daughter, who was a happy child, ready to make friends with Tom. She rarely saw her own father.

Then, only a year into their marriage, Tom's ex-wife became terminally ill and his two children came to live with them. Fiona found this a hard task: 'If they had been, say, two and three, it might have been easier, but they were already set in their ways and resented being with me. They were used to their own way of living, and because of their mother's illness they were very disturbed, unsociable children, rather wary – almost as if they expected a hard time. This was wearing for me. I felt I could not really love them. At times it felt like a duty, which in turn made me feel guilty. But it was so much easier to do things for my own child. Mind you, having been an only child she was pleased to have siblings, but they were never nice to her and she was hurt. She had expected them to be sisterly towards her, but they were not outgoing, loving people.'

What a hard task everyone in that family had to face. The young children, plunged into a new life while still full of grief; and Fiona, having to summon up all her patience and compassion in order to recover from the shock of their sudden arrival. She speaks very honestly of her experience:

'I think we made a lot of mistakes – Tom took his children away from boarding school, thinking a day school might be easier for them. I suppose the real trouble was that I was not used to bringing up boys, and this one was now 12, not an easy age. And although Tom's two children were very close to him, he was not much help for he considered it my job to look after them. It was a lonely time for me – none of my friends had stepchildren so there was no one really to chat with. I always felt guilty, under great stress; felt that they needed more affection than I could give them. I knew in my heart that I didn't really want them there. I felt truly sorry for them, but it was hard to have enough patience – which means that guilt is there all the time.'

Fiona, whose life as a stepparent has been so much more full of responsibility than she had anticipated, has given great thought to her role: 'One thing people don't think of, is that when stepchildren come to you, *you* have not chosen their names – they may have names you would never choose yourself. And of course they are not a bit like you. I am blonde and they are very dark. When I took them all out shopping, or to the playground, people would remark on this, which they hated.'

4
Settling into the New Family

Starting a new relationship is exciting, and when you reach the stage of finding a home together it seems as if your life is suddenly under control – you know where you are heading; this is the beginning of a new world. Then you remember the children! If you or your partner, or both of you, already have a family, then you know that at least some of your past life is about to come into that 'new world' with you:

> Although she already knew, Mary told her daughter that her friend Polly was coming to stay with them every weekend: 'She can share your room, won't that be lovely!' Her daughter was indeed excited at the thought of her best friend coming. What fun! But why was Polly's daddy coming too? He was not nearly so much fun as her own daddy, who she only saw once a month. Polly's daddy never played hide and seek with her. And Polly was different now too: 'She's rude to my mummy and says she can't cook pasta properly!'
>
> Mary's dream of a new world faded fast. She realized that settling into a new family set-up was going to take a long while. Most of all, she realized that the past would always be with her: 'I must have been naïve, I suppose. I was only thinking of my own happiness and that of my daughter. And here she was – miserable. And here I was with a stepchild who was obviously growing to dislike me – and my pasta!'

> Amy, a schoolgirl whose own father had died, had no difficulty in accepting James as her stepfather. 'He never wanted us to take his name; he knew we wanted to keep our own dad's name. He said it was important for us to have our real dad as a role model, not him. We have now created our own family, which I think is better than many real families. I have several friends whose parents have separated, and with their live-in dads it is frowned on if they do anything wrong. I feel sorry for them.'

Frank was another stepfather who understood that he had to consider the children's feelings when he moved in with them. 'When we first got together, my new partner wanted to create what she called a normal family situation. She wanted our new unit to be the stable, recognized one. She was trying to blot out the past (which she called the wreckage!) and expected her children to look on me as their dad right from the start. Her ex-husband may have been impossible to live with, but I sensed that the children did not feel the same way. I know I would have freaked out if some other man had wanted to be called Dad by my children!'

David, when he moved in with a new family, said he found it hard to know what his role was. He had not married his new partner, so that 'our house was full of names! I remember we had four surnames between us at one time. My partner's children call me David. We call ourselves a household, not a family.'

'My present wife is a stepmother of course, as I have two young sons, but she never calls herself that,' says Morris. 'She has had no severe tension, only a few domestic squabbles like any birth mum might suffer! We still can't decide what the boys should call her. I like the French words – belle-mère for stepmother, and beau-père for stepfather.'

There is no actual job description for a stepparent. It is a role thrust upon anyone living with another parent:

'Settling in is not how I would describe our start as a stepfamily,' said Sally. 'It was more like squatting!' She had moved into her partner's home and found herself in charge of two young boys. 'Their father was working long hours, even at the weekends, and their mother would turn up while he was out. She obviously resented me, and managed to make the boys feel the same way, though she had never looked after them properly and was only supposed to have limited access. I found it so hard living in their father's house, and I couldn't go to work because I had to look after the children. And they knew how to manipulate me and their dad – even though they were still young, they could be quite cruel. We lived in a small village where everyone knew each other, and the youngest boy would sit in the trolley at the supermarket and call out, "She is not my mother, she is taking me away!" Luckily everyone knew me, but I found it hard to laugh at the time. Children can be very destructive.'

Sally and her partner have survived for they both believe in trying to be positive rather than negative, and they now have two sons of their own. 'Yes, you do feel a different love for stepchildren,' says Sally. 'Love of course, but a different love, just as you have a different type of love for everyone – parents, siblings, friends, and so on. But if you don't like children, then don't embark on a relationship, stay apart. Apart from anything, it is sheer hard work!'

Most stepparents agree with Sally: it is hard work. And as Jim says, 'The trouble about stepparenting is that you have to go on seeing your ex-partner – if it were not for the kids, you could leave them out of your lives.'

Mike found other problems about settling in to his new life with a mother who brought three children with her, while his three were living with their mum: 'The hardest part was trying to show affection for my stepchildren – who were fairly accepting of me on the whole – while feeling guilty about my own children. Their mother kept telling them that I had deserted them, and I so longed for them to know that I still loved them.'

It is important for the children to get to know each family member, and be able to recognize and accept all the different relationships between them. It is not always enough just to introduce your new partner to the children – they will have aunts, uncles and cousins as well. And as one six-year-old pointed out, 'You never said you had two dogs!'

When only one partner has children

Of course, when a new partner has no children of his or her own, there are no such worries. However, if this is a man, and his partner has been a single mother, her children will not be used to an adult male in their household. 'I remember resenting this strange man coming into our lives,' said Julie. 'My sister and I gave him a hard time – never letting him be alone with our mum, and telling our teacher that he was nothing to do with us when he came to fetch us from school. I wonder that he put up with us for so long – about two years I think it was, before he left.'

A senior family therapist confirms that such resentment towards a single mother's new partner is not unusual: 'Of course, living with a single parent can have some negative effects, but a child – especially an eldest child – will have been given more responsibility and done a lot of sharing. The mother may well have depended on that child for emotional as well as practical support. So when a new person comes into the mother's life, it alters the child's privileges as a partner and a friend.'

If your new partnership was the cause of your divorce, or your partner's divorce, then resentment from the stepchildren is almost inevitable. They will have suffered from the separation and possible loss of one parent – their emotions are still raw: they may have a sort of love-hate relationship with their parents who they blame for this awful disruption in their lives; they may even be blaming themselves in some way – children often feel guilt when a family breaks up. And now these children are expected to accept a new adult into their lives. One senior family therapist found in her research among stepfamilies that children who have already experienced a parental divorce are more likely to fear an incoming stepparent than those who have lost a parent by death. If they have suffered from quarrelling and even violent parents, they naturally have very real fears that such behaviour might recur in a new marriage. It is no wonder that many such children are never able to relate positively to a stepparent.

Becoming a stepparent to bereaved children

Many stepfamilies do find it easier to settle if one parent has died, rather than following a divorce, but such a situation naturally does bring its own problems:

> My friends said becoming a stepmother would be easier for me because my partner's ex-wife had died, so I would not have her breathing down my neck. But I suppose I never gave much thought to her children. After we got together, though, I realized they had not had enough time to mourn the loss of their mother, and seemed to think that their father had forgotten about her.

'How can you love this lady? Don't you love Mummy any more?' I heard one of them say to his father. My partner and I both tried hard to keep their mother's memory alive, but it began to seem as if she was too good to be true. How could I ever compete with this wonder woman?'

Maybe this stepmother had rushed into marriage with her new partner before he and his children had had time to grieve. It took time for her to understand that she and her partner could never replace a happy marriage: 'Eventually we had to create a new, quite different relationship, but it was still very hard for the children to accept me.' This is something that all therapists stress: a stepparent can be an additional parent, but never a replacement parent.

If you marry a widow or widower, they may still be grieving, still carrying a lot of anger – and, of course, if they have children there will be a great deal of worry. They have had to cope with a child or children on their own, which can mean they are tired, tense, perhaps even overwhelmed. Usually it is better *not* to avoid talking about their lost partners – most widowed people love to talk about them, as do the children. Pretending that they never existed and being embarrassed to mention their names never makes for a relaxed atmosphere. Your new partner may feel guilty to be loving someone else anyway. 'Am I betraying my first partner?' is a common thought. And the children may be appalled at the thought of their parent loving someone new. Great sensitivity is needed at such times.

When Lizzie moved in with her new husband, a widower with two children, she found his late wife's clothes still in the bedroom cupboard. It needed all her understanding to appreciate how difficult he had found it to move them – and she gently persuaded him to help her explain to the children that keeping all the photographs of their birth mother around was a much happier reminder.

If a widowed parent marries a divorced parent, they will not have had the same experience when they decide to settle together with their families. For one thing, the bereaved children will have only the one, possibly new, home. The other children will still have their old home as well as the new one. This can cause an immediate friction between the step-siblings: 'You're lucky, you can see your dad every weekend!' 'Just because your dad died, why do you have to share mine?' 'I don't want yours, so there!' The squabbles can continue for a long while. Diane remembers when her father married a widow with a young daughter: 'She was the same age as me, and she got all the sympathy as her dad had died. No one seemed sorry for me when my dad left my mum – I loved him so much.'

When it is a mother who has died, it can be very difficult for a stepmother to help the children:

> I felt so sorry for them, a boy of nine and a girl of seven. Their father never talked to them about their mother, and I suppose this was why they never talked about her with me. If I asked them about her, they refused to answer, as though she was a forbidden subject. It was quite a frightening experience in a way. I felt almost as if their mother's ghost was around – as if she had never been a real person.

This particular stepmother found that the boy was the first of the children to accept her into the family – although initially he seemed full of anger, which sometimes took the form of kicking his bedroom door down or breaking things in the kitchen. The little girl took much longer to relax unless her father was around. However, after a while she began to talk about her feelings. She was able to tell how she also felt angry that her mum was not around any more and that she did not ever want her dad to marry anyone else. 'I realize now,' said her stepmother, 'that I probably tried too hard. Not that I was trying to replace their mother, I only wanted to help them remember her.'

If a new partner does gain the trust of their stepchildren, they need to show respect for their mourning. Perhaps by accompanying them on visits to a graveyard, remembering the date of a dead parent's birthday – and of course always allowing the birth parent to spend an anniversary day alone with the children. (Remember poor little Margaret, who was not even allowed to display her photos of her mother.)

Talking things over before creating a new family

Talking things over is the best way to resolve so many of the problems facing stepparents trying to settle into a new life. And the talking should begin long before moving day. Because, as psychologists often point out, talking is not necessarily *communicating*, which means exchanging feelings and emotions. Time is needed for true communication – you can't expect a few talking sessions to relieve everyone concerned of their anxieties. Each family has to get to know all about each other's former difficulties, and any traumas they have been through. The more relaxed an atmosphere you can create with each other, and then with the whole family, then the more stable a foundation you will lay for your new partnership. Also, if you can talk about (and, if possible, introduce) members of the extended families – explain how the varied relationships work – the children will feel more at ease. It is very important for them to get to know the full situation: whether their home and lifestyles are likely to change; whether their parents will be able to continue caring for them.

It is worth repeating here that children must always be told the truth – however stark that may seem. Perhaps Mum has a new boyfriend, perhaps Dad has to go to court, maybe Gran has a terminal illness – children would rather know the truth. You may recall the stepmother who was told she had to 'create a history' for herself and her new partner? Family therapists agree that it is essential that anyone contemplating the blending of two families is aware of the two histories involved. They point out that past emotional experiences, especially those of the children, have to be understood, for the impact of these experiences – i.e. marriage break-up, confusing relationships that have been going on within a family, acrimonious behaviour or unresolved grief – can all be brought into the new household. The negative effects of these experiences may continue to disturb children for many years to come.

Trying too hard to love the stepchildren

Suzannah knew all about conflict:

> Talk of settling into a new family makes me want to laugh – now that I've stopped crying. My two children stayed with my ex-husband every weekend, but my new husband's three girls stayed with him most of the time as their mother had a high-flying executive job and was seldom at home. When I first met them

they were friendly and seemed happy to meet my two. But after I moved in, they seemed to turn into monsters. They were bad-tempered and disobedient, refused to go to bed until their father did, behaved badly at mealtimes – the youngest boy even used to throw his food on the floor – and the two girls were rude and spiteful every time I spoke to them. And my husband never stuck up for me. I think he thought it would be disloyal to his children. I felt he was being very foolish as the children were becoming so spoilt. I also got the feeling that the girls thought I didn't like them, which I certainly did. No, settling in was not the right description for that first, dreadful, year as a stepfamily.

Poor Suzannah – but this is not unusual behaviour when children are faced with a new person in their parent's life, as well as other children coming into their home. Suzannah continued: 'I knew they were just trying to draw attention to themselves, that they resented any woman taking their mother's place. But there I was struggling to reassure them, to do everything I could to help them, when I would so much rather have been looking after my own children – it was a living nightmare.'

The children's father said that they had never been so difficult before: 'Perhaps they're just trying to point out that they lived here before you!' This may well have been true, but was of little help. Even when there is a loving relationship between the two adults involved, they have to have respect for each other and their families.

So how did Suzannah ever come to terms with her situation? Did the two families ever settle? Her answer was similar to that of many stepmothers:

> I gave up trying to be all things to all of them. I stopped struggling to love my stepchildren as much as I loved my own – how could I? And strange as it sounds, the children all helped (all five of them) – they sort of formed a little group, possibly to get away from all us parents! And once they were happier and stopped resenting each other, everyone seemed to calm down. I'm not saying it all happened overnight – many a week went by when I wanted to give up – but now I feel we only have the same number of problems as natural families!

SETTLING INTO THE NEW FAMILY

Second weddings

When we talk of natural families, most people will assume we mean married couples and their children. In fact, of the 350,000 marriages that take place each year in Britain, one in three is a remarriage for one or both of the partners. The decision to marry is of course a complex one for many couples. Can we make a go of things a second time round? Does starting a stepfamily involve too many responsibilities? What will the children say?

For younger children, their parent remarrying can finally put paid to all dreams of their birth parents getting together again: 'Does that mean you'll never live with Mum again?' Teenage children often tend to become moralistic about a parent's live-in partner and feel more comfortable with the idea of marriage. 'We didn't like Dad having his girlfriend in the bedroom,' said Philip. His sister agreed, explaining that 'somehow it seemed to reduce the status of marriage. Mum always said it was important.' Other parents, such as James, say living together with the children before getting married is a good idea: 'It all becomes easier with time and helps everyone to get used to the idea.'

So much to do with the planning of a stepfamily has to be played by ear. Mothers who wait until their children are happy to say yes to their remarriage tend to be criticized by other stepmothers. 'What happens if they say no?' they ask. This does tend to suggest that it is not always wise to ask a child's 'permission' before you remarry – although your life will obviously be easier if they support you. Whatever the circumstances, it is right to tell the children in advance, all together if that is possible, and preferably not the night before the event is due to take place! It is worse still if you wait until after the wedding. Kevin's father phoned his son one evening to say casually, 'Remember Mandy who you met in the park the other day? She and I got married last weekend.'

The wedding day

Once you have made the decision to remarry, you may find that the wedding plans – even for a quiet civic ceremony – are not always as straightforward as you had hoped, for you have to remember, as one therapist remarked, 'When it is second time around, there will always be another person in the marriage.' In fact, there may well be two other persons – ex-partners that is. This all makes it harder for the children. Dad may well want his child to attend, but the child's mother may be horrified when she hears about it. 'Do you really want to go and see Dad marry that girl?' she may ask the child, and so his or her loyalties are split in two directions. This is so unfair on children, and all you can do is to let them decide for themselves and then not be hurt by their decision. If children do want to attend the wedding, make sure they feel part of the day:

> Sadly, eight-year-old Alison was given no part to play in the arrangements for her widowed mother's marriage to Grant. Alison had known Grant for many years, and liked him a lot, and was not expecting life to change after her mother had married him. But on the wedding day, Alison felt very lonely. She was not made to feel part of the ceremony; she just sat with some friends in the church. That night her mother told her she must put away her photos of her own father. That really hurt Alison, and from that day on she felt a tremendous sense of loss – although at the time she did not truly understand the reason. She still liked Grant, they were good friends, and at times she even called him Dad. But it was as if she had lost her relationship with her mother and lost her old life.
>
> When her mother and Grant had a daughter, Alison was never jealous of her half-sister and they became good friends. But Grant often talked about blood relationships and made it clear that they were the ones that mattered most. This made Alison feel that he did not love her so much – that he would be loyal to his own family, not to her.
>
> Even today, as an adult, she feels that slight barrier between them. 'Does he still love me?' she wonders, and retains a great sense of divided loyalty. 'I have moments when I only want to love Grant, which makes me feel disloyal to my real father. It is hard not to feel that way as I was only two when he died and I can't really remember him. I think maybe my mum hid all photos of my dad in case Grant's family did not like to see them. Only many years later did I go with her to visit my own father's grave, and it was the first time she really talked about him. I think she was wrong not to have mentioned him to me before – but I can understand her feelings.'

Even in a registry office, a small child can carry a posy of flowers, and older children can be given small tasks – like ushering in guests or handing out service sheets. However, the day will need careful planning. We all know relatives who can be easily hurt over tiny details concerning the arrangements for a first wedding. Even more complicated still are the plans for a second, when it is far easier to upset members of either family. Mandy said: 'We invited every relative we could think of in our two families, from grandparents downwards, so that no one was forgotten. It was up to them if they didn't want to come.'

Bob's sons were teenagers when he arranged his wedding to his long-time partner, Janet. The boys were pleased, both asked to be best man, and both wanted new suits. But their birth mother was angry and it took a great deal of persuasion before she would let them attend. Janet's own seven-year-old daughter was looking forward to the day as if it were a party, until one of her school friends came up with a worrying remark: 'So you aren't really born yet if your mummy is only just going to have her wedding!' At once Janet realized that her explanations about divorce and stepfamilies had been sadly inadequate!

Brenda wondered if her new partner's discussions with her future stepson had perhaps been over-explicit. The teenager appeared to have accepted the future arrangements and insisted on coming to the wedding, 'So I can drink your health.' And this he did, in no uncertain terms, at the reception. 'To my dad and both his wives!' he shouted as he downed the champagne. His father finally had to take him home, and Brenda had her first experience of a teenage stepson (see Chapter 8).

Clare's day was a happy one: 'The children all wore their best clothes, my parents managed to be polite to Geoff's parents, and even my ex-mother-in-law turned up – she brought us a present!' Such a scenario is not that unusual – although several families admit that after the wedding, some of the smiles came off with the party dresses: 'Does it mean we have to call you our stepmother now?' or 'My mum was a much prettier bride than you!'

Tessa's three young children were happy to be included in the wedding plans, although daughter Lesley was upset that it was not a large church wedding: 'It was in a little hall, so I was upset I couldn't be a bridesmaid.' But not only did they attend the wedding, all three children went on honeymoon too! 'We had three nights in a posh hotel,' said six-year-old Ted proudly!

5
Guilt, Jealousy, Resentment and Anger

All these powerful emotions can stem from divided loyalty – one of the toughest problems parents and their children have to face following a family break-up. And when a new, or step-, family is created, loyalties can be switched around with tragic confusion.

Most often, it is loyalty to an absent parent that causes such agony for a child. Remember how the only father figure in Alison's life as she grew up was the man who became her stepfather, and how even now in adulthood she feels she is being disloyal to her natural father. 'Should I be loving another man more than him?' she asks herself.

Malcolm, the father whose wife ran off with their two-year-old son, finds it hard to reconcile himself to his son's loyalty to his birth mother:

> My son is now 12, and old enough to realize that his stepmother has been his main carer for most of his life. He has great respect for her. He also knows how mercilessly his own mother tries to brainwash him into believing that his stepmother and I are wicked. She upsets his holiday plans, she is always deliberately late for her access visits, she refuses to meet his school friends, and takes no interest in his school activities. Yet he remains incredibly loyal to her. In some ways I admire him for it, but I find it hard to explain.

David clearly remembers such feelings as a young boy:

> 'My father had several relationships after he and my mother divorced. And I never wanted any contact with any of his partners. He always had more to do with his partner's children than with me and my brother and sister. We all grew up in a family where we didn't talk to each other. When they first parted, Dad actually did talk to me, but I lived with my mum. Both seemed to feel the need to explain things to me. But it was a bit late by then – and I kept everything each of them said to myself. I

would have felt disloyal to talk to anyone else about it.' That strong feeling of silent loyalty stayed with David for many years, resulting in him seeking counselling as a young man, when he – not surprisingly – found relationships hard to handle.

A conflict of loyalties is a cruel legacy of family division, and yet the tug of biological ties is often overwhelming. Guilt, though, is often an emotion that arises from these bitter conflicts.

Guilt

We've already seen guilt within so many situations – from a natural sense of shame at personal behaviour, to a sad belief that you and you alone have caused your family's conflict. Most parents feel guilty at some stage of their separation if it means breaking up their children's home: 'Should we be doing this? Would it be better for the little ones if we stayed together? Should I inflict a new parent figure on them?' These age-old questions cause varying degrees of guilt in men and women.

Guilt can become a lifelong emotion for someone whose childhood has been shattered by the adults around them. Joanna's parents used to fight a lot, and yet she and her brother were never told that their father was leaving. When he did, Joanna felt an enormous guilt: 'Was it my fault? I know I often tried to butt in to their conversations; I know I annoyed my dad. I expect that's why he went to live with that other lady.' What a sad thought for a small child, but it is not an unusual one. And Joanna admits that she still carries that guilt inside her today.

Marjorie, now in her fifties, still feels guilty about trying to spoil her mother's wedding to the charming man who became her stepfather: 'He never tried to act as a father, and always spoke well of my own dad, but I nearly wrecked their marriage. Yes, I'll never get rid of this awful guilt feeling.'

Many women say that for many years they have suffered the same guilt feelings as Marjorie. But is this only a female issue? I've met stepfathers whose emotions at losing touch with their children have plagued their lives. It is inevitable that a father will feel guilt when a separation makes it appear that he has abandoned his children. '*I* should be looking after them, not their stepfather,' said Rex. Sometimes it is competitiveness that causes guilt in a newly created family. Paul found himself buying toys and clothes for his children that he could scarcely afford when they visited him on their brief access days. 'My ex-wife then made me feel guilty of trying to buy their love.'

All this guilt among parents can give stepchildren a feeling of power – they *know* you are feeling guilty and trying to win their love, and so they can – and do – manipulate you and your partner. And yet among the children themselves there is great deal of guilt hanging around: 'Poor Dad is living all alone in a flat while we're in this big house!' Even at eight years old, Maria felt guilty. Sandra felt guilty when her stepmother was giving her far more attention than she was giving to her own daughter: 'She was an artist and helped me with my great love – painting – but she was ignoring her own daughter. I remember feeling horribly guilty, just as though it was my fault that she was being left out.'

Jealousy

Jealousy is closely associated with guilt. It is also an insidious emotion – hard to bear and hard to conceal. According to the organization Relate, 'Jealousy is a major hazard of second families, rooted as it always is in insecurity.' This is understandable, for who can feel secure when they discover their partner now loves someone else? And how can anyone feel secure knowing that they themselves have betrayed their long-time partner? Only when you are confident in a relationship can jealousy have no hold over you – occasional envy maybe, but not the green-eyed monster!

It is when one parent takes a new partner that jealousy rears up in a child. He is unlikely to admit to such an emotion, but may well show it in various ways of behaviour – usually aggression, tearful withdrawal, or spiteful actions towards a sibling:

> Mark's mother died when he was only six months old, so he became very close to his father. Then, when he was ten, his father remarried. His new wife had no experience with, or liking for, children. She made it very clear that Mark was to be seen and not heard. She accused his father of treating the child as a baby, and

would never let him have bedtime stories or play games in the garden. Mark remembers being in London and his stepmother was angry with his father for taking the boy's hand to cross the road. 'But what I remember most of all,' he said, 'was being kept out of everything they did together. I became more and more jealous as she made my dad take her for drives or to the cinema or a restaurant and never let me go with them.'

Another small boy, Nick, spoke of his own mother's jealousy of his stepmother:

'She would ply me with questions when I visited Dad and his new wife. "Has she got a bigger sitting-room than me? Has Dad bought her a new car?" It got so bad that I hardly dared tell my mother anything.' Soon Nick began to feel jealous himself, and started to refuse to visit his father.

What neither Nick nor his mother realized – and would probably not have believed possible – was that the stepmother was also jealous! Like other second wives, she felt somehow second-best: 'I was very young, and desperately in love, and wildly jealous when I realized my new husband couldn't give me his full attention. His ex and her son were always there in the background. I wish someone had warned me that taking on a man who is already a father requires more thinking about than my own selfish needs.'

What is difficult to remember, as many therapists point out, is that the birth mother will probably be suffering far worse jealousy. Imagine your child being cared for by another woman. Imagine them having fun with her rather than with you, perhaps going on holiday together. Such thoughts, especially for a mother living on her own, can turn into real fears. 'I'm sure the children will prefer their dad's home now there are two parents there – a sort of real family atmosphere – not just me on my own.' As a stepparent you will have to remember that you are not the mother and cannot replace her. Your jealous feelings, though, will probably never be as strong as hers. (We should probably exclude here the tiny minority of women who, for whatever reason, intentionally desert their children.)

Equally strong feelings of jealousy are often aroused in birth fathers and stepfathers: 'How come he gets to see more of my own son than I do?', 'Why does my partner give more time to her son than to me?'

Step-siblings

Step-siblings can experience many emotions, but often suffer from jealousy, mainly of one another. When two families are suddenly joined together, 'blended' is not usually the word to describe their new situation. One leading child therapist agrees, stating that, in most circumstances, 'Blending is an unrealistic description.' Children who in other circumstances might well make friends, find being rearranged into a new family unit causes tremendous friction. A great deal of attention-seeking behaviour occurs in the younger ones, and sometimes even violence in older children: 'My son threw a plate at his stepbrother one day! The trouble was I always hesitated to punish, threaten, or even admonish my stepson for fear he would never like, let alone love, me – or my own child. All stepparents I talk to say the same thing: with your own kids, you know they understand you will always love them even if you are really angry, or lose your temper, with them.'

This stepmother is far from being alone in her feelings. When a child has lost his place in his original family – perhaps he was the eldest, or was a rather spoiled youngest – he will be deeply hurt and become unreasonably jealous. Ruth said:

'This happened to my twins, Guy and Genevieve. When I split up from their father, I joined up with a new partner who had three children – one older than the twins, and two younger. They obviously felt squashed into a kind of non-place in the family and became increasingly troublesome.' Only with a great deal of co-operation from her partner and from the twins' father, who agreed to care for them every weekend, did Ruth restore order to the new household. She admits she should have explained more to her children before the move. 'If I had told them what to expect – perhaps made them believe they would be very special, and given them certain responsibilities towards the younger children, they would have accepted the situation. I've learned so much the hard way!'

You will recall that Suzannah felt the same way, and was finally able to relax when the step-siblings in her family got together, realizing that they were all in the same boat, and that it was their parents who had caused all the jealousies in their lives!

A common cause of jealousy between step-siblings can be overcompensating behaviour by one or other of the birth parents – usually the non-resident parent. They bring lavish gifts for birthdays and Christmas and then the other children living in the same house feel left out. Many stepparents tell me that when they first joined their families together, they decided to give all the children an equal amount of pocket money: 'This saved an enormous amount of jealousy!' That sounds like good advice: make sure you are being fair to your children – they are sure to find out what the others get!

Of course, even natural brothers and sisters can feel jealousy towards each other – one may do better at school than another; one may be a parent's favourite. But even stronger feelings can emerge when a half-brother or half-sister is born into a new family. 'When my half-brother was born,' said Josh, 'I was 12, and rather embarrassed by the whole baby business. Everyone began to make a fuss of him, as if I didn't exist any more. All the aunts and cousins brought him presents and just ignored me. I began to feel stupidly jealous. And it was all made even worse because I was expected to look after him a lot of the time!'

One young girl was very jealous when her father had two sons by her stepmother. Her natural mother soon realized that her daughter assumed that her dad thought more of the boys than of her:

> She always had a strong relationship with her father and still needs him. Now in her teens, she rings him up and asks him to take her out. He was slow to recognize that need in her, and was not giving her enough of his own time. When I pointed this out to him he began seeing far more of her. I realize we could have avoided a lot of her jealousy if we had talked these things through when we first split up.

It seems as if all family members can be smitten with this wretched emotion. Helen's memories of settling in with her new family are of being filled with jealousy:

> It seemed to be everywhere. I was jealous of the time my new husband spent with his children; the children were jealous when

he spent time with me; one of his daughters became jealous of my son who was musical, and so could play piano duets with her dad. There always seemed to be rivalry between them, but I suppose that happens within all families. My husband and I are very close, but we realize that there is no natural bonding between me and his children – you have to work hard at your affection for stepchildren and not let jealousy get in the way.

Helen is thinking along the right lines. She has to do all she can to let go of the emotions that could destroy her relationships with the children, and concentrate on the love she has for her husband. She knows she is loved and valued in return, and is now beginning to understand that they both have enough love to share with all the children.

Resentment

Defined in the dictionary as 'indignation, bitterness or ill-will', resentment includes all these emotions within many stepfamilies. It is a feeling directed towards an act, situation, or person. The acts of divorce and remarriage; situations such as bereavement, loss of a parent or home, sudden abandonment; persons within a family who cause these acts and situations – all of these engender strong feelings of resentment.

Stepmothers who find themselves expected to care for a household of children without help from their father, and with constant abuse from their natural mother, are perhaps the most likely people to resent their situations: 'I wish I had never agreed to live with him and his horrid kids!'

But what about those horrid kids? They may well be resenting their stepmother and her insistence on tidy rooms and prompt mealtimes, and the fact that she has 'stolen Dad'. Other children, such as Gail, will be extremely resentful of the fact that she and her brother are living with their mother and her new husband in a large house, while their dad is living in a bedsit in the next town: 'It's not fair, I know that Dad pays for us, and I'm sure not going to call Mum's husband my stepfather. I feel so uncomfortable with him in the house.'

Many fathers also feel resentment about such situations. Stepmother Lucinda said wistfully, 'My ex-husband resents the fact that I have found happiness in my second marriage.' The organization Families Need Fathers talk of many fathers who have every reason to feel resentful of the outcome of their separation or divorce, now exacerbated by one or more stepfamilies. Their members consist mainly of fathers fighting for contact, and they stress the need for equal responsibility for the children: 'My ex-wife expects me to pay the full Child Supplement and yet never lets me have the 50/50 parental responsibility that I am due. But it is not the money I resent, it's the fact that she tells my children I don't want to see them. And all the while they are living with another man – it's heartbreaking.'

Conversely, one ex-wife had a different story to tell:

> The arrangement is that my children's father is to take them out every Sunday, and yet week after week he is either late, or doesn't turn up. I suspect his new partner is the problem, he's so weak when she's around. My youngest son cries every time, and his school work is suffering. The older two are beginning to resent their once beloved Dad, and to say that they don't want to go out with him any more. I can understand how they feel, and it is really hard trying to get them to stay loyal.

Often the bitterness starts during the break-up of a family – and the children may well carry this on into the new household: 'We resented our stepfather from day one – I suppose we never gave him a chance. But seeing him with our mum was so hurtful, and he never let us be alone with her.' Once again, it seems that so many of the emotions and problems have not been resolved within each family before they get together. Within a bereaved home, or one in which divorce proceedings are underway, it is not easy to face up to the future. But if some of the problems can be thrashed out, some of the emotions acknowledged, then not quite so many bitter feelings will be carried into a new family. For bitterness can smoulder beneath the surface for a long while, before finally turning into aggression.

Anger

A well-known psychiatrist writes: 'In stepfamilies, unexpressed or unresolved anger from a previous marriage or family is likely to prevent new relationships from thriving.' Certainly, when your

GUILT, JEALOUSY, RESENTMENT AND ANGER

partner is still fighting with her ex-husband it is hard to remain supportive without getting too involved in a way that might exacerbate the situation. Pippa was fortunate in her choice of a new partner:

> I have a very strong relationship with my present husband, so we can withstand the stress. My previous husband was a frightening person, eaten up with anger. He had been gone for a year (I had left him) when I met my new partner. A year later, my ex-husband found a new wife and now we are all sort of friends. I was very surprised at the anger I had in myself. Then, at the end of the day, I came to realize that hate only harmed me. I couldn't vent it on anyone else and suddenly it came to me that I was not doing myself any good. And my new husband gave me some self-value again.

It is perhaps worth noting here that if you talk of hating a person, you still have feelings for that person – you've exchanged love for hate. Indifference is the true opposite of love. Once you can feel indifferent towards a person you once loved (still caring, but not loving or hating), then you will have separated emotionally.

Some ex-partners find their anger harder to deal with as they get older: 'My dealings with my ex-wife are entirely conciliatory and obsequious (she thinks I'm over it), but I still have a lot of anger. We co-operate coldly, and only when necessary because of the children.' That father, still angry over his first marriage, is barely able to control his feelings in spite of great understanding from his new family. For such parents, the anger – which began over arguments with their first partner – is still festering. Counsellors from Relate suggest that a parent should try to understand what has caused their anger. If you can calm down (and, if possible, talk it over with a friend), consider if you have ever felt like this before; and, if so, how did you manage to overcome it? Often it is the result of being in a situation over which you felt you had no control – maybe a separation, maybe a death. After any loss, reactions can be painful, even violent. You can feel angry towards the lost person, angry at those who are left, angry at yourself. Panic sets in, you may start shaking.

Talking of situations over which you have no control – think how powerless your children must feel in the same circumstances. They may be bursting with anger; it's no wonder they have become aggressive and unpopular among their peers. Children certainly pay the price of listening to fierce rows between their parents. It is scary when the professionals talk about anger left over from childhood, but we should listen to them. Anger, if suppressed inside, can lead to depression in adult life.

Researchers at the Centre for Family Research in Cambridge have found that boys tend to be more aggressive in these circumstances, whereas girls are more likely to lose confidence and withdraw into themselves. They explain that a small child may feel he is going to be abandoned if he hears arguments going on between his parents that make him feel neglected. He has good reason to be angry.

If you can explain to your child that you are also angry, you may both be able to free yourselves of the feeling together, and at the same time save him from carrying the burden of anger into adulthood. Physical exercise is one of the best ways to do this. Depending on the age of the child, swimming, kicking footballs, climbing hills, chopping wood or painting the garden shed, can all help to get rid of aggressive feelings. Helping to scrape the wallpaper off the bedroom walls is surely better than resorting to violence and bullying in the school playground! You may also discover – as with so many methods you use when trying to help your children – that you are helping yourself at the same time.

Stepmother Pippa says that she was surprised at all the anger she had inside her. But when it was pointed out to her that *all* the children in the house were fighting, she felt vindicated! Stepfather David made the same excuse: 'One of the children has an explosive nature – anger and rage frequently break out. It made me so angry that one day I slapped him.' This is not an unusual situation in any family – the children are furious with each other, and so you argue that your anger is all their fault! It is all very understandable, but in newly created households it is essential for the adults to remember that most of the anger will have been left over from a previously unhappy time. Said Dick: 'I've learned to bite my tongue!'

According to an American paediatrician, Dick is probably using a sound parenting skill. Answering angry words with more anger only turns everything into a power struggle.

Andrew soon realized this when dealing with his difficult stepson:

'Even when he grabbed me by my shirt I never hit him – to my relief! I know if I hit him I'm in the wrong – you can't win that one – however angry you feel.'

When the children are not your own it is wise not to overreact, and to be sure to condemn the angry words and actions, but not the child. Perhaps you can point out that in your house everyone is treated with respect, and that you never talk like that. When her young stepson suddenly blurted out a torrent of abuse directly at her, one mother forced herself to keep quiet. Getting no response from her, the boy repeated the foul words, but soon grew tired of shouting and took himself off to his room. Later that day, when he spoke to her quietly about his homework, she thanked him for his respect. Such a method does not always work, but within a new family it is a good idea to make clear how far you are prepared to let the children go.

Deirdre was having problems with her stepdaughter's anger, which was being directed at her young half-sister:

> I was at a loss to know how to cope, but with all the anger around in our house it was vital to get help. The counsellor at a Children's Clinic helped me enormously. She told me I must see things from my stepdaughter's point of view. What were the good things about her? Was early evening perhaps her special time that she remembered with her own mother who had died? Certainly that was the time when she always began to upset my baby's bathtime, even throwing things at her. I had to learn that I must not take everything too personally, but say to myself, 'Hey, I'm the adult here!' I was also taught some basic skills such as listening, keeping my mouth shut, being assertive and so on. I have never regretted it, our home is a far more relaxed place now, and I truly think my stepdaughter is a happy child.

6
Keeping the Peace – Family Rules

Most households are formed by two people who have decided to live together. They gradually merge the experiences of their own childhood homes and build up a lifestyle for themselves. When the children come along they accept that style as normal. But, however conventional many lifestyles appear, each one is unique, as anyone trying to unite two households will discover.

Rebecca, her husband and four children lived in a rambling, shabby house on the outskirts of a county town. A cosy kitchen was the main living area, where relays of meals, family discussions and children's games all took place. The real living room was seldom used, except by the dogs who enjoyed the faded rugs and shabby chairs. Bedrooms were filled with music blaring and unmade beds; the bathroom was in constant use; the front door was always open on to the pram-cluttered hallway.

Jenny's and Keith's small terraced house was filled with books. Every table, chair and shelf was laden with stacks of academic books, with no room for flowers or ornaments – even the bedrooms (and sometimes the beds!) were covered with books, files, or papers.

Anna's flat was straight out of a Sunday newspaper supplement – white carpets and settees, glass tables, and under-floor heating. The kitchen seemed to be made entirely of stainless steel, with shiny metal blinds and a mosaic-tiled sink.

George and Molly and their twin sons lived in a semi-detached thirties house on a run-down estate on the edge of a large city.

Imagine all these widely varying family lifestyles merging together. Yes – every one of them, and many more besides, are doing just that all the time. Academic Keith is trying to get used to living in a house where his stepchildren use books to build boxes for their guinea pigs, or just to colour in. Anna's stepson appears every weekend with a pile of dirty shirts, demanding bowls of cereal and baked beans on toast at all hours of the day. 'Don't you ever clean the shower?' she wails on finding her state-of-the-art bathroom turned into a football changing room.

Now consider the children who are suddenly uprooted from a

familiar home and plunged into a different atmosphere. Remember the little girl who moved with her mother into her friend's house? For her, nothing was ever the same again.

So how do stepparents come to terms with a new lifestyle? For some, it is a constant battle of wills – either keeping the old ways or giving in to the new. Compromise is often seen as a weak move, a feeble sort of surrender in an era when assertiveness is the order of the day. But is making concessions in order to settle your differences a weak idea? Not many marriages – first or second – could survive without it. Without compromise, most live-in relationships come to grief.

Janey is finding a clash of lifestyles hard to cope with: 'I live in a tiny cottage in the country, and when my partner's sons come to us each weekend they hate having to share a room with my ten-year-old. Also, they're used to suburban living, so that "What can we do?" is their constant cry, and their father has to spend the whole time driving them miles to the nearest cinema.'

In a more affluent household, accommodation will be less of a problem. Everything will be much easier if the children can have their own space – perhaps even their own bedrooms. But for many this is not physically possible. What is important for children is that they eventually come to see not only the house they are living in, but also the house of the 'absent' parent, as their home. One may be a house where they have a room to themselves, the other may be a flat with only a cupboard in which to store a few of their books or toys. Yet if they can be helped to feel happily 'at home' in both, they will enjoy a far more secure childhood.

Even more disturbing for a child is when they have to move to another country. The new way of life, apart from the language problem, is hard to cope with. 'My little girl was taken by her mother to live in Spain,' said Brian. 'I do now have contact, but moving from an English seaside town to a Spanish country village has been quite a shock for her. When she comes to visit me she gets very excited, and though she now speaks Spanish, she says she does not like her stepfather's house as none of the furniture is like mine!'

Greg admits that when he married his partner and brought her and her young teenage son to live with him in the south of England, the boy found it very hard. 'It was probably the biggest trauma for him – moving from his comfy home in the Midlands,' said Greg. 'He had to come to a new, smaller house, go to a new school, make new friends, it was very hard for him. He wanted to phone his own dad every day, obviously needing that contact with his old home. He became hyperactive, and we feel sure it was partly due to the move.'

Bridget was also taken a long way from her old home on the south coast when her mother married Joseph, a farmer from Wales. 'I think Bridget found it very difficult,' Joseph said. 'She used to go down south for her holidays, but I could see it was hard for her to come back each time.'

James said his house was also full of tension when his stepdaughters moved in with him and their mother. 'It meant the girls were uprooted from their happy primary school, and had to go to the local school in my town. It made me realize how important a settled home is for children.'

It is important never to let a stepchild feel like a guest – they must feel at home as quickly as possible, and when they are older have their own keys. The 'host' family too must be helped to understand that they will not be given less attention now that the house is full.

Of course, the ideal is to move together into a new home – create neutral territory. This makes it easier for both families, especially if you include the children when house-hunting. Then they can help to choose their room. (If they can't have separate rooms, then let them each have some private space, even if it's only a cupboard for their precious things.)

After an unhappy home life, a move can sometimes be a relief – and even when coming from a loving home, a move can be exciting for a child if it is well handled. Sarah was the child whose mother decided not to make a direct move out of the old and into the new all at once, which made their move easier for her daughter:

> I don't even remember leaving our old home. One day my brother and I went to school and in the afternoon we were picked up by a friend, where we stayed the night. We enjoyed that, and then the next day after school Mum fetched us and took us to our new home – so it never seemed dramatic. And best of all, we loved the new cottage. We had two rooms up in the attic, so we felt independent.

Conflicting lifestyles

Of course it is not just an unfamiliar location that makes the transfer to a new family home difficult. It is the unknown atmosphere and lifestyle that can make for a traumatic upheaval. Just because two people want to spend their lives together does not mean that their families, and their accustomed ways of living, are going to be totally compatible. Far from it! Each partner is going to bring attitudes and values learned from their birth family as well as from their first marriage. It is unlikely that all these will mix comfortably together. The underlying cause of the breakdown of many second marriages is the irreconcilable difference in the partners' attitudes to life, standards, and values for family living. All children grow up accustomed to the day-to-day habits within their own families, so it can be a huge challenge for two families, each with its individual habits and rituals, when they decide to live together.

'We clean our teeth in the kitchen', 'We open our Christmas presents before breakfast', 'The dog sleeps in my bedroom' – these are minor things, but they may be different from those of the family you are going to live with, and are sufficient to cause difficulties – ranging from mild irritation to serious conflict. This is when a family's ability to talk honestly and openly will be invaluable. And again, the advice of family therapists is worth listening to. They say that the only way to cope is to accept the other family's habits and rituals, while at the same time acknowledging your own unique (and perhaps equally irritating!) habits. This is a daunting task for stepfamilies, but many have followed this advice and have managed to blend together – and have even come to laugh about their eccentric habits as well!

Joy and her three children were used to a carefree style of living, one that could be termed 'hand to mouth': 'We muddled through, and if we had to live on baked beans at the end of the month, I never worried – I knew I could always get a job as a typist if things got desperate.' When she moved in with Robert, whose life was never in a muddle, Joy and her children found his routine quite restricting: 'I adore him, but he expects meals on time – imagine! And when his daughters come for weekends they are shocked if I forget to make the beds or don't do the washing-up every night.' Trivial things maybe, but they represent totally opposing standards and, as such, could ruin a relationship. However, Joy decided to let her stepdaughters arrange the weekends to *their* timetable, while insisting that *she* remained in charge of the planning of outings and casual meals every other Sunday. In time it worked, and even Robert had to admit that she had managed to combine two lifestyles with amazing success.

It does seem that it is usually the stepmother who has to smooth the path towards a workable way of living together. However, Joy was not complacent, and added: 'Considering that we keep hearing from the media that children from stepfamilies are three times more likely to run away from home than children from natural families, I reckon we're perhaps luckier than some families.'

Faith knew nothing about such statistics when she first moved in with Ken. Her husband had taken off with a new partner the year before, leaving Faith with their two sons who were eight and ten years old. The older boy, Neil, had taken over the role of father, and was shocked when Faith told them she planned to live with Ken. She thought it would relieve the boy of the responsibility he felt, and allow him to enjoy his schooldays without worrying about his mum. Ken welcomed them all and behaved as a natural father – taking them to football matches, helping with homework, and buying them new sports gear. But when Ken offered to teach Neil to skate, the boy blurted out, 'No way!' Faith and Ken tried not to show their disappointment at this sudden rudeness, when both Neil and his brother had seemed happy with Ken.

Wisely, Faith ignored that particular outburst, but over the next few months Neil would have sudden fits of sullen behaviour, even anger at times, which he took out on his mother and younger brother. Ken became impatient: 'We've been too soft, what he needs is some more discipline!' Faith contacted her ex-husband, but he blamed Ken and said the boys were never badly behaved when they visited him. Neil had more and more temper tantrums and then one day he did not come home from school. Faith became very worried: 'It was a nightmare, we had to get the police, and his father came and I thought he and Ken would come to blows. Neil was found within 36 hours, but it was an experience I don't want to go through again. His father wanted him back, but to my surprise Neil refused to go with him. Ken wanted us to forget the whole episode, but I asked Neil's headmaster for help, and he suggested we see the educational psychologist. When the phrase "disturbed behaviour" was used, I was really scared. Neil was only 11 then, and I began imagining him growing up into a violent teenager. But the psychologist explained that he was probably still angry about his dad leaving home, angry with me for letting him go, and unhappy for us all at the same time. He was totally unable to reconcile the two strong emotions – anger and unhappiness.

'I began to see how terrible the confusion of emotions could be in a youngster's mind, knowing how strong they had been in my own. But what could we do about it? And why had all these tantrums suddenly started after so long? Again, the psychologist was able to explain. He said that even as young as 11, children never want to show how upset they are with any situation that is beyond their control. But every now and then they can't keep up their apparent cool and anger bursts out. Slowly I began to understand, and with the school's co-operation we managed to help Neil release a lot of his feelings – he joined evening judo classes, and went on a school trip to Wales for an outward-bound type of holiday. I suppose it was nearly a year before he was able to relax completely and become a normal, boisterous but happy young boy. But it was great – we were so happy for him, and I had learned so much myself.'

That really is what stepparenting is all about; as one stepmother said, 'My new family is a constant sort of learning curve. Some people call it a work in progress. We started with two adults and two children, then one moved out, but two more babies arrived and another adult appeared on the scene. It's always changing – I guess that's just family life!'

Different standards of behaviour

Yes, family life is never static, is it? And perhaps that is what makes creating some sort of order so hard. Organizations such as Relate, which are constantly in touch with families trying to unite several different lifestyles, acknowledge that when two households first move in together the problem that looms the largest is one of discipline: 'Who gets to tell them what to do can become one of the flashpoints for conflict.' They are right, and most stepparents agree with them – the trouble being that no two families have the same idea as to what constitutes discipline. One parent may see a child's behaviour as perfectly normal, while another will consider it to be out of control.

Within a stepfamily there is almost bound to be confusion as to who has ultimate control, and this can become a huge issue. One father may be used to being the head of the household and be appalled when his stepchildren refuse to listen to him. Another may be happy to hand over all matters of discipline to his wife, but will then find that his own children have no intention of obeying their stepmother. Once again, talking over such matters with everyone in the family is essential. The differences in values must be recognized, and if possible accepted. In other words, you will probably have to agree on certain ground rules: 'In this house we all help with the chores; no phone calls after ten o'clock; everyone has to eat breakfast before they go to school.' If the children are living with you only part of the time, it is going to be hard for them to find one set of rules in their mother's house and another in their father's. But if there are definite ways of behaving, they will get used to them and know what to expect. Stepmothers advise that you should discuss your ideas on how to run the household with your partner before you move in together – not rigidly, but outlining the ways you prefer. So when the stepchildren disagree (as they will!), you can both explain that that's the way it is in your home.

The main thing children must be helped to understand is that neither household is right, nor wrong; they are simply different. One mother, whose stepchild came from a different country, was able to say, 'That's the way we do things over here', and it was accepted without argument. You have to let the children know that really dreadful behaviour will not be tolerated: 'There are certain limits in our house – so that's that!' As in all families, if there are no ground rules, no set conventions, a child will feel insecure.

June's story describes such a case:

> My stepdaughter comes to us every other week, and when she first arrives her hair is in a mess, her case full of dirty clothes, and

she uses bad language. I used to get upset, sometimes angry, but I realize it is not her fault – her mother lives quite a different life from me. Over the week with us she changes completely. She becomes polite and tidy, she enjoys being with my children, and always thanks me for laundering her clothes. I sometimes ache for her, but she has accepted the two ways of living, and in a strange sort of way I suppose this is a security for her: she always knows what to expect.

In some cases, a child may be feeling unloved, and there is a real danger that she may lose her self-esteem. This is when a stepparent must try to be positive. She must find something good for the child to look forward to, not dismissing her sad past, but showing her that there is a lot to enjoy in life.

Stepmothers are often the ones who have to set the standards, although many would comment that that means keeping the peace! As Rebecca said:

> I worked very hard with my stepchildren, trying to get on with them as well as keep their relationship going with their mum. I had to act as a buffer between their dad and his ex-wife too, who hated each other. What with that, and at the same time trying to give enough of my time to my children and my new partner, life was not easy.

Helen feels that her husband gives too much time to his own children: 'I think my own daughter gets jealous – I know I do!' Celia, who has three stepchildren, also had to work harder than she had imagined: 'I was not always in agreement with my husband over discipline. I was rather like a mother hen and hated it if he criticized my children.'

Deirdre, who has no children of her own, has had some difficult times over her stepdaughter's behaviour: 'Mainly over small things, hair washing, baths, meals, and so on, which were obviously not done in her mother's way. But all these little routines became major problems. Luckily my husband backed me up over most things – he certainly did when his little girl wanted to sleep in our bed! He was very firm about that.'

It does seem that all such problems can be overcome if and when the two parents are in agreement, and so present a united front to the children. Stepfather Peter has found this within his family: 'It's having a really strong relationship with your partner that makes it all happen, all work. In spite of all the initial problems with discipline, and I admit I did lay down the law at times, I don't regret it at all.'

Many families have written lists of rules – one drawn up by the adults, one drawn up by the children. I quote here from two lists of rules devised together by several families:

Guidelines for stepchildren

- Try to be friends with your mum's or dad's new partner.
- Do not forget your stepparent loves your parent and will be feeling as anxious as you about the situation.
- Remember your stepbrothers and stepsisters are feeling as strange as you are.
- Try to behave in your stepparents' home as you do in other friends' houses.
- Do not compare your two homes too much – everyone is different and has different tastes.

Guidelines for stepparents

- Tell your children what to expect from your new partner – warts and all.
- Do not move a child out of her room for a stepbrother or stepsister.
- Give a child plenty of time to be alone with his real mother or father, and allow him to love her or him without feeling guilty.
- Try to be friends to the children, not surrogate parents.
- Do not run down your ex-husband or ex-wife – he or she is still your child's parent.

The two lists say it all really. Each member of the family likes to feel that they are allowed a say in the running of the household. We all know rules are made to be broken, but if parents and their children can discuss the pattern of their new lives along such guidelines, they will have made a good start.

Many stepparents, especially fathers, tend to leave all attempts at discipline to the birth parent. This is usually a wise move, but beware that the stepchildren do not interpret this as meaning you don't care about them. Ideally, if you and your partner can agree in principle on methods of discipline, then when one of you is absent, the other will know how to behave with the children: 'Remember what your mother said!' (Of course, if there is full co-operation with the birth parent on such matters, then yours will surely become a very successful stepfamily!)

James was determined not to demand anything from his stepchildren, but leave all the behaviour problems to their mother: 'But on a few issues of discipline I did feel I should be talking to the children. It all took a massive amount of effort, and at times it can seem as if you're losing – you know, when your patience goes! But they now say they appreciated my taking a stand, and of course their mum and I being in agreement is the secret.'

Greg, at 24, was not quite so confident when he married a girl who had a ten-year-old son: 'It is a large commitment, you can't relax any more, the child is always there demanding attention. There are no real problems I suppose, but I leave all the discipline to my wife.'

David also had no children of his own when he became a stepfather to two schoolgirls:

> I was not used to children, and the girls' feelings towards me would swing from one thing to the other. Apparently when their mother first talked to the children about my moving in with her, one of them said 'OK. He can move in as long as he cleans up the cat sick!' I had wondered what my role would be! On the whole they were tolerant of me, although from time to time they would say things like, 'Don't tell me what to do, you're not my father.' So I left all the parenting issues to their mother. I sort of followed her lead.

Nigel felt he had to make a stand with his stepson right from the start:

> He was a difficult child – not his fault, he had lived through his parents' acrimonious divorce and been in care for a few months – but he had a lot of temper tantrums. One time he was extremely rude to his grandmother and so I forbade him to come into the house until he apologized, which after an hour or so he did! When it happened again some months later I took the same firm line –

and it worked. We had no more major problems until he was in his mid-teens and opted out of school. He became a sort of hippy, refusing to apply himself to anything. As I was working hard to keep him, we had some stand-up arguments, and at 17 he left home telling us to get rid of all his possessions. We did not see him for the next six months. He was out of work for a long time after that, but he never lost touch with us and eventually came back and found work in our town and now lives independently in a flat and owns a car. We consider ourselves a successful family now – we are all very close. Our early troubles with my stepson did put a strain on my relationship with my wife, but we never felt the need for counselling.

Respect for each other's children

It is good to hear of relationships that are not spoiled by the children. However strong your love for each other, as a mother you will have to help your children to feel respect for their stepfather, just as a father will have to help his children respect their stepmother. Tell your partner when you feel you are growing to like their children, that you have their interests at heart, and are trying to understand them. It all sounds so simple, doesn't it! But many stepparents are managing to work towards a real understanding of each other's families, and assuring those just starting out that it is all worthwhile. Despite the pitfalls, there *is* an upbeat side to stepfamily life! This is confirmed by several professionals who, although they tend to meet only the families in need of help, find that children from stepfamilies are often better equipped to deal with life today. To quote one experienced child therapist: 'Stepchildren learn to cope in a world where nothing is for ever.' Think what they have experienced: break-ups, remarriages (sometimes more than one), several losses, possibly including that of a parent, and so they have learned to cope with a great deal of disruption in their lives. In the future, hopefully they will be able to cope with the various problems that life presents them with.

7
We're All in This Together

Many stepfamilies draw up a family tree, so that all the members can learn how many people are on every side of their complex families. For very young children, this could actually be in the shape of a large tree, with many branches indicating the various relationships and colour photographs of the close family members. One teenager remembered: 'When Mum and Dad both remarried it was hard to understand who was who in all the families until Dad put up this drawing of a huge tree in our playroom. I remember it was quite fun working out which granny belonged to which branch of the tree!'

A new baby in the family

It is when a newborn baby, the offspring of the new partners, is added to the tree that the other children can see how two branches can be truly united. However simple that all looks on a chart, it is not always the happy event the parents had hoped for. For a start, it is a very large, and personal, decision for a couple to make especially if each partner has a different view.

Jessica, who has three children of her own and three stepchildren, had strong, if somewhat cautious, views: 'I think it wiser not to have a child with a new husband, which might cause new problems. I know that stepfamilies only work if the children are kept in the picture and are happy with the set-up. I don't believe it would work well if two families are involved, and you try to create a third by having a child together.'

Stepmother Celia agrees:

We also have six children between us and I feel we were right not to have a baby. I did want one at first, but my husband did not – saying one family would go one way, the other would go the other way – so where would the baby go?! He was probably right. I remember one time when I called all the children together because I wanted to talk to them about our au pair who was not much use – and apparently they had thought I was going to tell them I was pregnant! They all sighed in unison, 'Good, no baby!' I was glad we had made that decision – and I bought a dog!

There can be other reasons why a decision is taken not to have another child, as you will see from Raymond's story, which is rather different: 'My partner and I both had children, but as my ex-wife refused to divorce me for five years – and as we have old-fashioned ideas – we decided not to have our own baby until we were married. By the time we were able to, we felt we were too old.'

A father is sometimes inclined to feel that he is being disloyal to his own children if he starts a family with a new, younger partner, as Laura found out: 'I have two stepchildren, and am not sure if I want any of my own. I think I do, but my partner is not so keen, he's done that! A big decision for him – maybe we will have just one.'

Another father had worried over how his six-year-old stepson felt when his half-brother was born, but the boy now says: 'I remember being excited, as I had never had a younger brother before.'

Conversely, Lucinda was the reluctant one when she remarried: 'I already had three children, my youngest being six. After such a break I was not sure I wanted more children, but my husband did, so we now have two more sons. It was quite an effort! But the siblings, surprisingly, were not jealous – perhaps because of the age gap. They all get on splendidly.'

Jenny's story is also an encouraging one: 'My stepdaughter often used to plead with us to have a baby, and she was ten when I had my first child, a boy. I let her hold the baby, and even take his pram round the block; she was excellent with him and loved him.'

It is good to hear when families do succeed in truly uniting in that way. Many stepparents confirm that a new baby has brought the family, including the stepchildren, closer together: 'We had one child each, and somehow having the new, mutual baby made life easier for them – it made them realize our level of commitment; they knew we would never leave them.'

Sometimes it is not so easy. A new arrival can cause a lot of jealousy in the family – a young child will feel upset that she is not now the youngest; many siblings fear that their birth mother will no longer love them; others feel their absent parent has been betrayed. You will recall Deirdre, whose stepdaughter's own mother had died:

'It was when my own babies were born that things became a bit hard. My stepdaughter had several tantrums, and would throw things at me when I was feeding the babies. I had to get help from a family clinic.'

Another mother, who had three sons of her own and two stepsons, was sure her new baby would unite them all: 'It might have done if the baby had been a girl,' she said, 'but they all got together to see who could think of the worst name for a boy! But in a funny way,' she added, 'it did sort of unite them – perhaps because they saw how upset I was – and now they all get on better than before, and take turns to baby-sit.'

Of course, there is often jealousy within natural families when a new baby arrives on the scene. But understandably, stepparents feel under greater pressure to prevent such emotions, feeling somehow guilty about the situation: 'When our son was born, I knew my eldest child felt the limelight was being stolen from him and I longed to protect him.'

Let's hope Peter is more fortunate when he says, 'My partner has two teenagers and we are thinking of trying for a child, and the two children think it's a good idea.' Kevin's story should encourage him: 'My stepchildren were teenagers when my partner and I had two of our own. They love their new brother and sister, the two boys have become close, and the two girls took to the little girl. We both believe in large families, the young ones learn from the older ones – the children grow up more balanced and able to hold their own.'

A new baby brings new understanding

Christopher's emotions were not unusual: 'I would do anything for my three stepchildren, and yet I felt a difference when my own son was born – a close feeling I can't describe.'

When a young girl becomes a stepmother, she may find it extremely hard to like, let alone love, her partner's small children. Jenny said:

> I had no idea how to cope with them. Naturally I didn't feel like their mother, more like an older sister. Now it makes me cringe to think how young and inexperienced I was, and how ridiculous it was to feel jealous of my husband when he took them out without me! When I first said to their father I thought I'd like a baby of

my own, he warned me it would change our lives for ever – but I didn't really believe him. Then when I had a baby of my own I had to ask myself what I thought about my stepchildren. I still didn't love them in the way I loved my own baby – and yet I was very fond of them. After I had two more babies I had much more understanding. I began to give more thought to the other children – and also to their birth mother. Until then she had never entered my thoughts – I never felt guilty at having taken her husband from her. Now, of course, I can understand her feelings. I can also see how my husband felt when sometimes he refused to get a baby-sitter for his children, saying he wanted to look after them himself. I was just the same with my first baby! In fact, I became rather a reclusive mother, but I really had few problems with sibling rivalry.

Sometimes children are unable to express their true feelings at the time, or perhaps, like Lesley, they don't want to: 'I was a bit upset when I heard the news that Mum and my stepfather were going to have a baby, but I didn't tell them at the time. Then when he was born I was besotted with him. I had to be careful not to talk about him to my own dad though.'

Rebecca was the stepmother who said she treated all the children equally, and that meant that she frequently ticked off her stepson, Johnny, when he was a typically reluctant schoolboy. It was only when his half-brother became a teenager that he realized how fair his stepmother had been. 'When you used to shout at me,' he told her, 'I thought it was because I was your stepson. But now I see you shouting at my half-brother, I realize you treat him the same way!' Rebecca knew she was forgiven by Johnny when she received a birthday card from him addressed to 'My Second-best Mum'. This made her conclude that 'the best thing about being a stepmum is that they love you for yourself, not because you're a mum'.

Teenagers

We all know how hard it is to be the parent of a teenager, but to be dumped into being the stepparent of a teenager can be traumatic! Parents who have had this experience stress that all they can advise is that you show an interest in their lives – not intrusively, but learn who their friends are, and always welcome them in your home; find out how they like to spend the hours out of school and what games they play or watch; make sure you give them their own space when possible. They will be testing you out – seeing how far they can go over such matters as to what they wear, how late they stay out, the language they use. If you can find a friend from another stepfamily who has been through this awkward time, this may be your greatest help. Meanwhile, never forget that most teenagers are streetwise these days, and consequently think they know it all! This does not mean that they are all rebellious, all on the drug scene, or going to be violently abusive to you or your children. But they may enjoy embarrassing you, take pleasure in reminding you that they have their own birth parent, and possibly even blame you for the present situation. After all, they are at a vulnerable age. Growing up is hard enough without having to take on parents' problems too. It is obviously essential that you agree to teenagers calling you by your first name – certainly not 'Mother' or 'Father'.

Of Celia's four teenage stepchildren, the girls were the most difficult:

> I suppose because they were more emotional – they would pour out their anger or go to their father in tears, so that he thought I was cruel to them, which I certainly was not. Then when they visited their mother, they were really abusive towards her partner. The boys were not so bad – well, they used to get into trouble at school – one was nearly expelled, and they used to fight with each other, but they were never abusive to me. We tried going to counselling as a family, but in the end I think what helped them the most was talking with other teenagers.

Sexual problems in teenagers

The above is good advice – if your teenagers can talk with their peers, they may not feel so isolated within a new family. For remember, this is a time when their hormones will start to kick in. If the children are teenagers when they first come to live with you, try to find out if their birth parent has discussed sexual matters with them, and be prepared to face awkward situations yourself. It often happens that the step-siblings are of different sexes, and during adolescence may try to avoid each other. A boy may well be attracted to a stepsister or, more worryingly, to a half-sister. As a stepparent you are going to have to instil great understanding in all the children regarding living arrangements. Firm limits will have to be set on codes of dress and undress within the family, and this is when parental example must come to the fore. It may well be helpful for a child from an unloving home to see how much you and their parent truly care for, and respect, each other. One stepchild told me, 'It was the first time I had lived in a house where the two adults really loved each other.' However, seeing your parent love another partner is often distressing, especially when you are reaching the age when you are thinking about members of the opposite sex. I've heard teenagers say that their parents' divorce has put them off marriage for life, while others (usually girls) say they want to find a partner and get married as soon as they can to get away from a stepfamily. 'But I'm worried,' said Gail, aged 17. 'Who will give me away when I do get married? My dad says he doesn't want to see my mum any more, yet he'll be hurt if I ask my stepdad, won't he?'

Another situation frequently overlooked, but all too common, is that of the father who is living away from his own adolescent children. Richard's story is a typical one:

> My first wife and I married when we were very young and, not surprisingly, we split up while still in our early twenties. We had the usual joint custody of our son, Karl, but as he was only six, we agreed he should live with his mother most of the time. I moved into a flat and it was arranged that Karl would come to me every other weekend. But after less than a year, she took him to live in the north. It worried me that I would not be able to see my son so often, but it was worse than that. His mother hardly let me see him at all. I wrote to him, but never had any letters back, and his mother even cut off relationships with my parents, so poor Karl lost his grandparents. The only time I involved any type of help, i.e. social services, was when the decree nisi was arranged, and I drove up to put my case – to no avail, but at least I had had my say. I still felt a strong bond with Karl, who is like me in many ways – we have the same interests – but he has been brainwashed by his mother and still won't be friends with me. Now that he is a teenager, I would so love to be able to talk with

him; I know he has lots of anxieties and I dread to think what his mother has told him about me. Visiting times are severely restricted, and very tense occasions. I feel sad – not just for myself, but for my son who is missing so much in the way of family life.

George is more fortunate in that although his son is living overseas with his mother and stepfather, he has an amicable arrangement with his ex-wife to share the cost of their son's trips to and fro between them:

> I see my son for several weeks during each of his school holidays and I have taken a part-time job so that I can spend as much time with him as possible. I am a strong believer that parenting should be a 50/50 responsibility. But I do worry continually that I am able to give so much more time to coping with my partner's youngsters (they are particularly difficult!) when I would dearly love to be helping with William. Now that he is a teenager, it is really hard not to be there if and when he needs me.

Teenagers arriving into the home may be even more of a problem when the stepmother is not much older than the stepchild. An adolescent boy will have his feelings aroused when his father brings a young, attractive girl into the family home. If they have just come back from honeymoon, he will probably be embarrassed to think of his father in such a role. Feeling very uncomfortable with the situation, he may well ask to live with his mother. 'I was very hurt when my son changed his mind about living full time with me,' said one father. 'I suppose I was rather naïve – or had forgotten what it is like to be an adolescent! It was my partner who put me right – and explained that Jim was far too embarrassed ever to be alone in a room with her. Now he just visits us occasionally when all the family is around, and thank goodness he has started to bring a girlfriend with him!'

More often, it is a young girl who is attracted to her stepfather. She may have suffered an unhappy time with her own father, and here is a kind man living in close proximity to her. She may innocently test her sexuality on this father figure who seems to like her. Parentline Plus, who offer help to all parents, say that they have calls from stepfathers asking for advice when a stepdaughter has been making advances towards them. And it is widely known that many teenage girls have to phone such organizations asking for help when a stepfather or stepbrother is sexually harassing her. Tragically, it is often difficult to know where the truth lies. One mother said:

> I found it hard to believe when my daughter told me that my partner was trying it on with her. Of course he denied it. Only after I walked out on him did my daughter own up that she had lied because she was infatuated with him, jealous of me, and wanted to hurt us both. I was devastated and ashamed of my daughter, and yet also unable to be angry with her. I could understand her feelings for my partner. I tried counselling, but it was no good – my partner never forgave either of us.

Abuse by stepfathers is a sad stigma that the majority of loving stepfathers have to bear, yet the tragic statistic that stepparents have also to bear in mind is that more sexual abuse of children is perpetrated by brothers or stepbrothers than by fathers or stepfathers. This is one very important reason for parents to create a household where every member of the family is able to talk freely, and be listened to. Sibling rivalry, as we have seen, can cause strong hostility and bullying, which, if not recognized by the adults, may well turn into sexual abuse. But what are the signs to look for? Counsellors suggest that moodiness, depression, ill health, and signs of withdrawal from others should all be taken seriously. Like adult abusers, youngsters who abuse can become manipulative, so if you suspect any doubtful behaviour, or a child gives any hint of a sibling hurting them in any way, they must be listened to, and professional help sought without delay.

If she is still young when she marries, a woman naturally wants her new partner to herself; needs to get to know him; needs to feel special. She may not worry too much that he has two children: 'Oh, they'll only come to us at weekends.' But perhaps having other young people around is not turning out as the young woman anticipated. She may feel that the offspring are nearly as old as her and therefore do not need parents anyway. But of course many of them do. They have come from tragically disrupted homes, suffered many losses, and still need adult supervision and advice. One girl clearly remembers her feelings towards her young stepparents: 'I was a teenager, struggling to come to terms with my own sexuality. The last thing I needed was to know about theirs.'

All parents, especially stepparents, should never hesitate to seek professional advice when dealing with teenagers. 'It was different in my day', 'I thought they had sex education at school', 'His behaviour is unreasonable', 'Why doesn't she listen to us?' All these concerns and questions accentuate the great divide between parents – even fairly young parents – and their adolescent children. Few parents ever come to understand that the arrogant behaviour of teenagers is seldom an indication of how they are feeling inside. Like their younger siblings, they will like to act cool, act sexy, while inside they are incredibly anxious and lacking in confidence.

Boys in particular are seldom able to discuss their feelings towards girlfriends, whereas girls are more likely to talk with their mothers about their boyfriends. Many stepparents do provide examples of happy relationships, which is something usually left out of sex education lessons in school. For teachers cannot possibly be expected to find ways of talking to their pupils about emotions, and they certainly do not have the time to listen to them. This is when parenting courses can give invaluable help and guidance, as well as introducing the teenagers to child therapy clinics and trained counsellors. One young stepfather said: 'Having no children of my own I found a Parenting Course very helpful – it was important to me to get it right. I learned not to expect the children to have the same relationship with me as they have with their real parents.'

Stepparents must never feel that seeking outside support means that they have failed in their role, or let their partners down. It shows that you care; that you have the strength of mind to discuss your anxieties with a professional therapist; that you truly want to be able to help your new family.

Barbara tried to help her two teenage stepsons while her own children were still toddlers, but found herself at a loss to know how to handle them:

'I thought they would like to be considered part of the family, so I asked them to baby-sit one day – but they refused. When I tried to treat them as adults they sulked, and when I offered to help them with homework they laughed – I began to hate it when they were around the house. And in fact they were around less and less. I never knew when they would turn up for meals, and although their father set a time for them to come in at night, they never obeyed him. Then one day they told us they were going back to their mother. I knew she was living with a very unreliable partner and would not welcome them back. And sure enough they were not allowed to stay with her.'

Barbara had many unhappy months before her brother, who is a counsellor, pointed out that the boys needed to spend less time with her and the small children: that it was as hard for them as it was for her. He explained that it is often wiser for fathers to talk to their sons on their own and that she should not feel inadequate. Now, after a lot of careful planning – their home being large enough to provide a sort of granny-flat division – the boys are able to lead independent lives. They get together at pre-arranged times during weekends, which they all enjoy. Barbara said, 'I realize now how hard it was for those boys, at such a vulnerable age, to see their own mother with a partner they could never relate to. And seeing how much their father loved me and my little ones naturally made them jealous. They have become so responsible and mature, and we've all grown up a lot in this last year.'

Awkward questions

If Barbara's stepsons found it difficult to understand how their birth mother could have chosen such an unreliable partner instead of their beloved dad, think about how hard it has been for teenage twins Ken and Kirsty. Their parents also divorced because their mother found a new partner: Roseanne. Their mother knew they would be upset, although they liked her new partner and got on well with her: 'But what do we call her? She's not a stepmother! What can we tell our friends?' They both went to live with their father, who gave them a lot of support: 'I was devastated of course, after 16 years of marriage, but I was determined to support the twins and not let it spoil their love for their mother.' A wise father, who was able to deal with many of the questions that his children did *not* ask him. So often when a lesbian relationship takes place, the children's father may tell them all sorts of ugly stories as a sort of bitter recrimination against his ex-wife, whereas Ken's and Kirsty's father said, 'It was their grandparents who gave us the most trouble. They objected strongly to the children even visiting their mother, and tried to influence them away from her. I suppose it's a generation thing.'

8
The Extended Stepfamily

The extended family is the name commonly given to all our relations: cousins, aunts and uncles, grandparents and in-laws. The word 'extended' can be rather an understatement when it is used to include a family's ever-increasing number of 'steps'. Perhaps the 'elastic family' would be a better name! One couple, who had been married for nearly twenty years, divorced – and both remarried. Their four children now have two more adults in their lives, and three half-sisters. They also have two more sets of grandparents. Their family is constantly extending, which for them has happily been accepted with few problems. However, many other families, as we have seen, do not settle so easily. Ex-family members are often rejected by their relatives, which can turn any future contact with children and grandchildren into difficult, even clandestine, affairs. And yet it is widely acknowledged that the extended family can contribute enormously to the success or failure of a stepfamily.

For Jim, it was his brother-in-law who spoiled his new relationship. After his rather acrimonious divorce, he married Lil, who was looking forward to meeting his family:

> My brother-in-law, who had been such a good friend, became really unpleasant overnight. He would not let his children play with mine any more, although the cousins had been great friends. I could see that he resented my split with his sister, but it was nothing to do with the children – why should he make them suffer? He really upset Lil too, who had few relations of her own and wanted to become part of my family.

Grandparents

It is usually the grandparents who are involved in helping to unite (or occasionally to upset) a new stepfamily. Following a divorce, grandparents have been known to refuse to acknowledge a new marriage or partnership. They may continue to talk as if the first marriage still exists and this can greatly confuse the children. And then, when a stepfamily is created, the grandparents may well find the new situation difficult to understand, let alone acknowledge. Even more than the parents and the children, grandparents will need a period of adjustment. Some of them find it very hard to identify with youngsters who are not their biological grandchildren. It is often this difficulty that upsets a future stepfamily.

When Louise went to live with Martin she knew that his two daughters loved his mother, their grandmother. Louise said:

> I was terribly hurt when she said that I was not welcome in her home. She made it very plain that their birth mother would be allowed there, in spite of the fact that it was she who had caused the divorce from Martin. I felt this was such a bad example for the children. After being with their granny, the girls would either ignore me or be very rude, almost abusive. I had not tried to act as a second mother, and was at a loss to know how to behave. Perhaps I was wrong, but Martin stayed loyal to his mother and so I decided to leave them. Truly, that grandmother spoiled what could have been a happy relationship.

Most grandparents, though, can and do contribute a great deal to the success of a stepfamily – just as their practical help is invaluable during and after a family bereavement or divorce. They can act as neutral ground for disturbed children: provide security (and not just in terms of finance) when a child can find nothing else of permanence in her life: 'Nan and Grandpa always used to pick me up to go and see Dad because he and Mum didn't want to see each other. They were great and never said anything nasty about my stepfather. I know they helped Mum a lot.'

Another grandmother had a different story to tell:

> My daughter had two boys from her first marriage and I saw a lot of them. When she divorced and remarried I naturally expected to go on seeing my grandsons. But my new son-in-law seems to think I'm redundant. He invites his own parents round at weekends, but makes it obvious I'm not welcome. I worry that he doesn't seem to care for the children.

THE EXTENDED STEPFAMILY

Families today do not always live within easy reach of each other as they did a few decades ago. 'Granny lives in Australia' is a familiar cry, and even when she lives nearby, she may well be working and unable to act as a carer or baby-sitter for grandchildren who are trying to settle into a new stepfamily. There are also those grandmothers who are jealous of their own children. 'I was never able to divorce my husband and start a new life like you have,' one mother said to her daughter. 'I stayed with your father and gave up the chance of a wonderful relationship – all because of you!'

Another grandmother was equally upset when her widowed son married a girl with three small children: 'I bet she is marrying you just to get a father for her kids! Or, more likely, just to get her hands on your money.' This particular woman does not sound as if she would make a good step-grandmother!

Grandmother Sonya was very worried when her son divorced and his children went to live with their mother and their new stepfather. She even went so far as to threaten her daughter-in-law, telling her that she and her son were going to demand custody of the children. Fortunately, her son and his ex-wife were both determined not to involve the children in any sort of custody struggle, and Granny finally mellowed and didn't carry out her threat. Many a son or daughter has had to explain to their children's grandmother that a second marriage is not necessarily second-best: 'It can be a new start – at last I have hope of a lasting relationship for myself and the children.'

Following a divorce, a mother often wants to split not only with her ex-husband, but with his entire family. It is understandable – but tragic for the grandparents and the grandchildren. Naomi left her husband, taking her twin sons and a daughter with her, and threw herself into her new role as stepmother. She completely ignored all her former in-laws. Her ex-mother-in-law was devastated to think she would not be seeing her beloved grandchildren, and frequently sent them letters and presents. However, these were all returned unopened. 'It broke my heart,' she said, realizing that the children were probably imagining that she no longer loved them. There are too many such stories.

We all know that not all grandparents are helpful or lovable – they may be the interfering sort, the over-critical ones, those who refuse to baby-sit, or those who grumble when they don't see the grandchildren every day! Within most families, though, the more contact there is with grandparents, the more everyone benefits – especially the children.

The generation gap creates a unique relationship between a grandchild and his grandparent. A child who seldom talks to his parents, especially a teenager who seems to grunt rather than converse, often talks openly to his grandmother or grandfather. When that relationship is denied, it is robbing both generations of a rich and stable part of their lives. Keeping up communications, if only by letter or phone, is so important. Even when children are living far away, they can e-mail a grandparent, and with their parents' co-operation can send videos and cassettes across the miles. That connection with family – with their roots – helps to give children a sense of security and belonging. And it can give their grandparents a new lease of life too! The Children Act emphasizes that all members of the extended family, especially grandparents, really do matter – although this is seldom enforced in practice. Legally, grandparents have little or no authority over the children unless they apply for Parental Responsibility (see Chapter 9).

Grandmother Patricia's daughter-in-law died suddenly, leaving her son with four small children. At his request she moved in with them and took over their care. For two years she became their mother figure: bathing them; cooking for them; taking them to nursery school; and reading their bedtime stories. Then, three years later, her son remarried, and promptly told his mother she would no longer be needed and must leave. He told his children they now had a new mother, and naturally they were devastated. 'We lost our mother, then our gran, it was scary!' was how the eldest child described their feelings. And the new wife, very young to become a stepmother overnight, found herself having to cope with a quartet of bitterly resentful children, all desperately missing their granny.

Conversely, since becoming a stepmother, Gillian has had to persuade her own parents to visit the stepchildren: 'My mother says they are nothing to do with her, and only comes round when it suits her. She and my father take no active part in the children's lives, and I feel as step-grandparents they could help them to feel much more a part of my family.' Many of these family prejudices could be avoided if parents and grandparents tried to put the children first. It may well involve trying to re-create friendships by swallowing a little pride – but, as Gillian says, 'Children grow up so fast– surely all the adults in their lives can provide them with a store of happy memories instead of stressful ones.'

Step-grandparents

Being separated from your own grandchildren can be distressing enough, but if you are then thrust into the role of a step-grandparent it can be equally traumatic. One step-grandmother described her feelings: 'I suppose I missed those sudden glimpses of how my own children looked when young – there were no family traits, no talents or eccentricities to look out for as there were with my own grandchildren – it was strange.'

Another step-grandmother called the children her 'pretend grandchildren', and then when a real grandchild came along only gave presents to her and not to the others. Young Ted was luckier with his four sets of grandparents: 'It's good, present-wise, to have so many!'

This is a time when bitter jealousies and rivalries can be aroused. What about the original grandparents? Are they going to be friendly? One step-grandparent said:

> We found it hard to love our step-grandchildren at first. For one thing, they told us outright that they didn't need us as they had some grandparents already! How on earth could we relate to them? We wanted so much not to hurt our son and his new wife, so we let the children call us by our Christian names and somehow that gradually broke the ice. We are now very fond of them.

A sensible idea – but one that some step-grandparents choose to ignore: 'My step-granny insists that we call her Grandma, and I don't want to. She doesn't seem to know we've got two grannies already, and I think she's hurting Dad too.'

Sometimes it is up to the birth grandparents to welcome the step-grandparents into the new family – to let all the children see that they are still loved and wanted. And if the step-grandparents can reciprocate and try to share their love among *all* the children, the new family will surely succeed.

It is often a grandmother who makes the family tree that helps to unite two families. I have seen a grandmother making two trees –

one for each family – and then asking a child from each family to add the new baby to their own tree. Even where there is not an entirely harmonious household, this sort of 'double entry' of a baby can spark a new feeling of oneness. Children begin to understand that their families are now joined together, but that each one has not lost its identity.

For one family, the new baby really did manage to unite what had been a rift between a young mother and a step-grandmother: 'My mother-in-law had always resented me and refused to come to my house, although she insisted on the children visiting her. Then when our baby was born she came running round the next day!'

When grandparents start their own stepfamily

A surprising number of grandparents are joining the ever-increasing list of divorcees. Some 12,000 people over the age of 60 get divorced each year in Britain. Perhaps they feel, as they reach retirement, that they want to stretch their wings – but in different directions to each other! Whatever the reason, it means that many grandparents are now finding new partners – and thus creating new stepfamilies. They may well be step-grandparents themselves, and are now complicating the family tree with several more branches! Extended families indeed. A teenage stepson was heard to remark, as he was counting up his growing number of grandparents: 'I don't know about steps – I seem to have a whole staircase of step-grandfathers and step-grandmothers!'

Such marriages, though, sometimes cause resentment among the step 'children', who will be adults, and possibly parents, or stepparents, themselves. They often have the same hurt feelings as a child, albeit with different worries: 'What about our inheritance?' 'Who will get the house?' 'Will they still give as much time to my children now they've got step-grandchildren as well?' Again, all these matters must be discussed openly with the (adult) children, and a solicitor may well need to be consulted.

The ex-partners

From the moment you take on the role of stepparent, you will be sharing your new partner with his or her children for the rest of your lives together. That means that you are also sharing it with those

THE EXTENDED STEPFAMILY

children's other biological parent. That parent will always be a part of your extended family – and as such must be respected. It is worth repeating what every family therapist emphasizes and many grandparents advise: no animosity must be shown between you and the stepchildren's natural mother or father.

Consider the biological parents for a moment. An ex-wife has borne your partner's children and was, after all, his first choice of partner. An ex-husband has known your partner longer than you have and is appalled at the thought of his children calling another man 'Dad'. How do new stepparents face up to these ex-partners? Are they able to develop a working relationship with them, or do they see them as rivals?

Carol has never had any problems with her stepchildren's birth mother, and this in no small measure is due to the fact that she has never tried to be a stepmother to them; she never uses the term if she can avoid it. Remember how she always referred to them as 'Alistair's children'. Carol said: 'From the beginning this seemed more natural as well as sensible, and now we are all good friends.'

Jean was another stepmother determined not to cause bitterness with her partner's ex-wife: 'Doreen and I have become friends and our children now play with each other. I think the reason we all get on so well is because my partner and his ex have been good parents, and always put the children first.'

One very young stepmother who gets on extremely well with her two stepsons had a hard time to begin with: 'Their mother would keep rubbishing me, and at first they believed her. I never said anything against her, and just sort of acted as a friend. I must have done something right because now they really do seem to love me and enjoy staying with us. I have been teaching them to read and they are great fun.'

An ex-wife or ex-husband who has not remarried or found a new partner is more likely to create trouble. One man said: 'My ex-wife is very bitter and hardly ever lets my son visit us, and she won't acknowledge that he has a half-brother and half-sister. She almost acts childishly at times. When my son told her that I would like some of my books back that I had left in her house, she gave them to him, but I found she had cut out several of the pages!'

William's ex-wife created trouble of a different sort, which his new wife finds hard to cope with:

She rings him up nearly every evening wanting some sort of help – fixing her TV or mowing her lawn and so on. I am looking after her two children during the week as she is on her own and working, while I work at home. So off William goes each evening, and at the weekends when he takes the children back to her she often gets him to do more chores. I can't believe it's right, I feel like a sort of childminder rather than a wife. But William says that I have to accept he's not exclusively mine! I wanted a child of my own, but now I'm not sure.

Christine said:

Our biggest problem was my husband's ex-wife. She told everyone I was trying to take the children away from her, and there I was bending over backwards trying not to say anything against her. I tried to keep the relationship going between the children and their mother, but goodness knows how many lies she told her children about me. She also tried to poison her eldest boy's ideas of his father with the result that he once ran away. When our mutual mother-in-law died she rang me to say, 'If you come to the funeral I will kill you!' I loved the old lady, so I went. I still include the children's mother in any family get-togethers, such as Christmas and birthdays, as I'm determined not to show any animosity between us.

But however understanding you may be as a stepmother, if your husband's ex-wife is unwilling to co-operate, there is little that you can do. Trudie said:

Although officially they both had Parental Responsibility, their mother took my husband's two daughters overseas with her. My husband was devastated, and although he loves our little girl, I can see how deep down he is missing his own children. And I am sure they must also be missing him, and goodness knows what their mother is telling them. The anomaly is that despite the prohibitive legislation now available, in practical terms it can be difficult to prevent a parent taking a child overseas. Some friends say I am lucky not to be saddled with stepchildren, but I would willingly share in their upbringing if only to see them and their father truly happy.

Trudie has good reason to be sad, but knows that no one can legislate for emotion. All parents who prevent their children from seeing their other parent forget that one day those children will want to know why they have been separated. More often than not, it is the birth mother who is guilty of such a selfish act, with the result that organizations such as Families Need Fathers have been set up (see Sources of Help).

However, it is not always ex-wives who cause such distress. Melissa's ex-husband took their two sons overseas three years ago following one of their regular weekend visits. Melissa is still desperate at the loss of her children. Her second husband spoke for her:

> There I was trying to be a good stepfather and understanding that the boys should have plenty of time with their birth father – and he goes and abducts them. When they were taken, we thought the law would be on our side. It was – kidnapping is a criminal and extraditable offence in this country. But it is taking all this time, and costing us all our money – for what? It seems unless the foreign government of the country they are in can recognize our government's rulings, we have little hope of success. It is breaking Melissa's heart.

Helen tells of another stepfather who is trying his best to help his new wife and her child:

> The trouble about stepparenting when you have kids of your own, is that you have to go on seeing your ex-partner. My ex-husband physically abused me for five years; he was an alcoholic. My new partner wants to protect me from him and won't let me take my son to visit his dad once a fortnight unless he comes with us. My son thinks this is ridiculous and they fight all the time. Meanwhile, my partner's ex-wife is very demanding – well, very greedy really – which means that we are suffering a lot of financial hardship.

Many ex-husbands, on their infrequent visits to their children who are living with a stepfather, tend to spoil them: 'He will bring them expensive presents, thinking that will make up for the many times he lets them down and forgets to visit. I have never prevented him coming – in fact, I am usually the one who has to arrange the times. Our son is beginning to see him simply as a sort of Father Christmas rather than a dad, it really upsets me.' An all too frequent scenario. A wiser one, however, than the fathers who feel it better to fade out of their children's lives altogether: 'They have a stepfather now, maybe it will confuse them if I keep turning up.' But what about children like six-year-old Jonathan, who keeps asking why his dad no longer comes to see him? Many a stepfather has had to explain to a bewildered child that his natural father still loves him, and that not all the father figures in his life are going to abandon him. For there is endless proof that children flourish best with continued paternal contact – however infrequent or unreliable. The biological link is all important. All of which confirms that a parent who withholds rights of access to a child who loves his mother and his father, is obviously acting out of spite, revenge or jealousy towards the ex-partner – without a thought for the wishes or needs of the child.

Tessa's first husband had left her, but when she set up home with a new partner he tried to move back in: 'He was very hostile to my partner and I had to get the police. Naturally the children were upset and wanted to protect their father. It was a difficult time, and we were determined never to criticize their dad in front of them.' Happily for that family, both Tessa and her ex-husband agreed that the situation was not the children's problem. They now stay with their father every weekend – he never lets them down.

Parental alienation syndrome

Because there is so much resentment and bitterness lingering between ex-partners who have separated in order to create new stepfamilies, an American professor of child psychiatry coined the phrase 'parental alienation syndrome'. Many other professionals are critical of having such an academic label for what is, after all, emotional discord between two individuals who share the parenting of a child; they state that the behaviour of an ex-partner does not necessarily brainwash a child into distancing himself from the other parent. In other words, these professionals insist that most children make up their own minds as to which parent is telling the truth. However, there is no doubt that the phrase does describe the bitterness that ex-partners often display towards their child's other parent. This can take the form of comparatively mild hostile behaviour, such as a mother not allowing her children to give their father her telephone number, to cruel cases where a parent tries to deliberately alienate a child from the other parent through lies and false accusations.

One teenage boy told me that his mother would tell him what to say to his father on visiting weekends. 'I knew most of it was lies,' he said. 'But I had to tell them to please her. You see, Dad had this girlfriend and being at his house was OK – she didn't try to be like a mum or anything. I guess Mum was jealous as she was on her own. But I wish she hadn't lied so much, she must have thought I was stupid.'

In its most cruel form, this sort of bitterness can drive a mother to allege child abuse by her child's father: 'My ex-wife twice resorted to such a charge in order to prevent me seeing my daughter. I was heart-broken, as I adore my child, and I know that she loves me. Naturally no evidence was found to support her wicked claims, but it was the worst time of my life.' You can imagine the feelings of that little girl's stepmother! 'I knew my husband was innocent, but we both felt that the very suggestion of abuse was humiliating. How could any woman be so cruel?'

All this acrimony between ex-partners that intrudes into a stepfamily makes any suggestion of settling down and creating a united family all the more difficult. It must surely be a strong reason why we hear of stepparents entering into third marriages. Surely these are the ultimate cases of hope triumphing over experience! But where is hope for the children? Let's take a brief look at the legal side of all these stepfamily relationships before we listen to the children's views on their ever-changing lives.

9
Legal Problems

The legal status of stepparents is particularly confusing and ambiguous, not least because the step-relationship has little standing in law. Indeed, under present British law, a stepparent has no automatic parental rights even in a remarriage where the children are permanently resident in that household.

The Children Act of 1989 states that after divorce or separation both parents (resident and non-resident) retain Parental Responsibility. If there is no major conflict between the parents (conciliation is the name of the game these days), and they have agreed on all the arrangements for their children – where they will live, how they will be brought up, holiday plans, etc. – a court will abide by their wishes and make no orders. Together with the Child Support Act of 1991, this legislation ensures that all non-resident parents continue to share responsibility for the children, whether in relation to financial support or general care.

This may sound good news for stepparents: 'No legal or financial obligations towards these children who are not mine.' Does this mean that you have no responsibilities whatsoever towards your stepchildren? Yes, but that means no rights either, which in reality gives you no say in any decisions, large or small, that have to be taken regarding the children's welfare and upbringing. This often starts some of the confusion, not to mention conflict, within a stepfamily: 'My three stepchildren have been living under my roof for several years. Naturally I am involved with them in many ways – they are sharing my home, and I treat them exactly as I do my own two children. I feel emotionally responsible for them if nothing else.' This man is expressing the views of many stepparents in his position. So what do they have to worry about?

The main difficulties arise when the step-partnership comes to an end – either through another separation or through the death of your partner (the child's birth parent). If you have been providing a home for a child for many years, you, as stepparent, might be called upon to continue with payments to the amount of the financial support you provided. And if you die, there could still be a claim on your estate.

So, a stepparent does acquire a certain amount of responsibility after all? This has become known as a grey area in family law. Any family facing such an ambiguous problem would be wise to seek sound legal advice. In the meantime, let's take a brief look at the meaning of the legal terms used when a family is making arrangements for the children following divorce or separation.

Parental Responsibility

Although the Children Act emphasizes that the extended family, including members of a stepfamily, does matter, in reality this is not always the case. Legally they have little or no authority over the children unless they apply for Parental Responsibility. So what does that entail, and how is it acquired?

A child's parents both have Parental Responsibility if they were married at the time the child was conceived or born, or if they later made the child legitimate by marrying, even if they are now separated or divorced. An unmarried father does not have automatic Parental Responsibility, but he can achieve it by:

- making a formal agreement with the child's mother without having to go through the courts at all;
- applying independently for a Parental Responsibility Order. Unless there are very good reasons for not granting Parental Responsibility, it is likely that any application to the court will be successful. Members of the extended family, such as grandparents or stepparents, can also be granted Parental Responsibility – but this does not take it away from the birth parents.

Residence and Contact Orders

Courts can make a Residence Order, setting out where and with whom a child should live. This automatically gives Parental Responsibility to any adult named. Joint Residence can be awarded to more than one person, allowing a child to share his or her time between the child's parents, or with another adult such as a grandparent, although this tends to be the case only in exceptional circumstances. A Residence Order would only be made if the people

LEGAL PROBLEMS

concerned have not been able to arrange things amicably among themselves, or via mediators and/or solicitors.

A Contact Order is only made by the courts if it is proved that a child would benefit as a result. This order emphasizes that a child has the right to have contact equally with both birth parents. It requires that the parent the child lives with must let him or her see the other parent (or guardian). Other relevant adults can apply for Contact Orders with leave of the court – e.g. grandparents. As we have seen, though, even a Contact Order cannot make either parent comply if they choose not to. In that eventuality, the court can also make a Prohibited Steps Order. This is to prevent a parent (or anyone else) from taking actions in relation to the child without the court's permission. (A parent with the Residence Order does not need to apply for permission to take a child abroad provided it is for no more than a month in any 12-month period.)

Another order the court can make is a Specific Issue Order. This gives directions about specific issues that one parent feels are essential for the well-being of a child – e.g. a particular type of education.

All these legal matters are likely to have been faced by a parent who has been through divorce or separation. So now that you are to become a stepparent, do you really need even more legal help? If you are wise, you and your partner-to-be should seek advice. There may well be aspects of your new relationship – not least of which will be the financial arrangements – that will need careful planning. An ex-wife still has to have maintenance money, and we have already seen how a father can resent his stepchildren while he is still having to provide for his own children who live with their mother.

Following an acrimonious divorce, Brian's ex-wife took his two children overseas. Naturally, he was devastated, and yet reluctant to resort to the law:

> Litigation tends to inflame things. However, I decided to get a Court Order which stated everything that my children were entitled to. [Remember, it is the children whose rights come first under the Children Act.] Once these were written down, my ex-wife finally did take notice of them. And now, although I hardly ever need to resort to using it, that order is still there to fall back on.

Brian's story is not an unusual one. Many mothers, on forming a new relationship, go to court stating that they want their new unit to be the stable, recognized, one. The mother wants to 'maximalize' the new parent, as one ex-husband expressed it. Obviously this would violate the rules of Parental Responsibility, and could damage a child by taking away parental permanence in his or her life.

Fathers too can forget their responsibilities, and change partners without a thought for their children:

> I have to plead with my ex-husband to come and visit his daughters. They still love him, but don't like going to his house because he has different women there each time – all of whom try to act like mothers, and my children hate that. He says he loves them, and brings them expensive presents, but when they get older they are going to realize that he only comes on visits when I arrange them, and even then he sometimes doesn't turn up.

When Jane got together with Keith, he already had a small child. She looked after the little boy for three years, when Keith suddenly announced that he had a new partner. Poor Jane. She said: 'I had grown so fond of the little boy, and he trusted me – we truly were like mother and son, a real family I thought. It was awful when he was taken away – Keith's new partner didn't seem nearly so caring. I feel truly bereaved, so think how the little boy must feel.' Jane had no official responsibilities towards the child, but even if she had been a married stepmother, she would still not have had any automatic legal rights.

Child Support Agency

This is a Government Agency, which was set up in 1993 in order to take over the responsibility for administering the payment of child maintenance. The Agency can require a parent who does not live with his children (known as the absent parent) to pay an amount of money as a contribution to their care. The Agency works out the amount of the maintenance from each parent's income and expenses. Even if the child spends time with both parents and they have equal responsibility, the parent who spends the least living-in time with the child is considered the absent parent. This does not apply to stepparents. In fact, the Child Support Act states: 'New partners of either parent will not be expected to pay anything towards the child support maintenance of children who are not their own.' Again, this does not seem to present any problems to a stepparent.

However, as most parents within second marriages are also stepparents, the financial problems can cause great difficulties, and in many cases real hardship. There are some tragic stories of families who cannot cope with the financial burdens, the most dramatic of which are often highlighted in the media. But there are many, many more ordinary, hard-working families who are having a real struggle to keep up maintenance payments: 'I love my children and want to provide them with as much as possible, but the Agency is asking me to pay an impossible amount and the burden on my new family is crippling.' It's an all too familiar cry.

Rose said:

When I married Arnie, I knew he had two children to support who lived with their mother most of the time. I have two children also, and my ex-husband is quite good at supporting them. But poor Arnie is having to struggle to pay maintenance for his two. Their mother refuses to work, although both children are in school, and so I am virtually having to work myself to help pay for them. We had planned to have a baby together, but now we don't think we can afford to – surely something is wrong here.

Yes, something is very wrong, and a stepfamily that shows all the makings of a happy unit, where there is a strong relationship between the 'blended' members of the family, deserves fairer treatment. Patrick and his partner agree: 'We wanted to get married and have our own children, but Patrick's ex-wife is constantly demanding more money and my ex-husband has disappeared, so I get no maintenance for our three children. As Patrick says, "Maybe two can live as cheaply as one, but five can't!"'

This stepmother obviously has a caring partner, but many stepmothers point out that it is wise to keep any money you have in your own name, 'or the ex-wife might claim it!' It may sound neurotic, but it can happen.

We know, though, that many stepparents are happily married and settled – sometimes so much so that one of them will consider adopting their partner's child. A stepparent can adopt a child, so that the child's status becomes the same as all adopted children and their rights are clear. But it is not encouraged. For, almost without exception, a child needs her own family history and origins – especially if a natural parent is still alive.

Adoption

There are many strange anomalies regarding adoption. First, it must be pointed out that couples who are not married cannot, as a couple, adopt children. This does not preclude single individuals from adopting a child, but a couple living together, however long they have done so, are not eligible. Also, courts are usually reluctant to grant adoption to a stepparent, unless there is no other way of achieving stability for a child. And curiously, the law states that, as a married couple, the natural parent and stepparent *both* have to adopt the child. Also, the birth parent must be over 18 years old and the stepparent must be over 21.

So why would any stepparent want to adopt a child? The only valid reason for doing so would be, presumably, to protect that child. If his natural absent parent is an abuser, violent, has disappeared or is in prison, there could be a sound reason. Also, if the other parent has died, the stepparent may feel a desire to adopt, thinking that the child's future might be at risk. They could, in such a case, take out a Residence Order, although this is not a binding arrangement. For, and this is vital to understand, *adoption is for ever*. No person can take that child away so long as they are loved and cared for.

So you want to go ahead? You will find that Social Services are always involved. Although a couple can apply to adopt after three months of marriage, Social Services are unlikely to support a stepparent adoption application before one year of marriage has elapsed. They have to produce a Schedule 2 report on the suitability of the parent and stepparent to hand to the court, and a report on the situation with regard to the other natural parent – for the other natural parent's consent is required, except in special circumstances. And Social Services will want to interview the children if they are seven or older, for they must understand what is happening.

It is essential that you talk to a child first, providing he is old enough, to make sure that he wants the adoption to take place. Even if you feel the adoption will safeguard the child's future, it will also take away his rights. It means that the absent natural parent will no longer have any rights over the child, and the child can expect nothing from him – the relationship has ended. You can see what a drastic step this would be. All children want to know their origins, where they come from, and why. Not to be told, perhaps until years later, is distressing. Children's feelings about their history, their parents and grandparents, can be powerful – you have to respect them.

If the father of an illegitimate child wanted to adopt, he knows that he has no rights. So he could not block adoption by a mother and stepfather. Only if a father can prove that he has played an active and ongoing part in the child's life can he be consulted. Otherwise, his agreement is not required.

However, even after learning of the difficulties involved, many stepparents do decide to adopt their partner's child, or children. Greg has a happy, albeit complicated, story to tell:

> When I married my wife she was divorced with a small son. However, he was actually the son of a previous partner of hers. To give him stability and a sense of history, and with the consent of both his natural father and previous stepfather, we adopted the boy. He was given the surname of my partner's first husband. This means that he cannot legally use my surname! But in fact he chooses to do so, and always uses it in order to be the same as his mother and me (except on any legal documents). My wife makes sure that the boy's natural father keeps in contact from time to time by keeping in touch with her former mother-in-law. We both feel this is right, so that after such a complicated start, he will always know his background. He has adapted (as well as adopted!) well and calls me Daddy Greg. There have not been any dissenting voices at all, and we both feel that in our case adoption was the best thing.

A change of surname?

Even if they do not adopt their stepchild, some parents choose to change that child's surname. Many mothers, whether married to their new partner or not, change their surname to that of their partner (unless they revert to using their maiden name). Then, because her child still has the name of his natural father, stepfamilies sometimes wish to change this, so that everyone has the same surname. In such a case the mother would have to get the consent of the birth father – and, even if this is given, the courts may not grant legal permission. They like to insist that the parents wait until the child is old enough to decide for himself or herself. Indeed, any child who has sufficient legal understanding may apply in their own right for the court's permission to change their name. In the meantime, there is no law that forbids anyone using any name they choose (as Greg's stepson has done) so long as they do not have criminal intentions! It is often when a child enters school that a change of name is used: 'I didn't want to change my name – I love my dad – but I felt better if I could tell my teacher that my mum and I had the same name.'

As with all legal rulings, there may well be changes in the law regarding adoption, and Parentline Plus has wise advice: before making any decisions about the future, talk it through with an adoption officer in your local Social Services department, or a solicitor skilled in family law.

The Children Act Family Courts Advisory and Support Service

Known as CAFCASS, because of its clumsy title, this is a new non-departmental Government Agency that will succeed the Family Courts Welfare Service. At the time of writing, it is due to come into operation in the spring of 2001. It is intended to bring fairer legislation to many of the controversial court rulings on child welfare and parental Contact Orders.

Drawing up a will

Another very important thing to discuss when making all the arrangements for creating your new family is the drawing up of wills. The word 'will' is almost taboo in many households, but so many serious difficulties can be avoided by facing reality before family tragedy occurs. When there are children concerned, it is a matter that must be discussed initially with your partner, before seeking help from a counsellor and legal advice from a family solicitor. Bearing in mind the rights that you and your partner may or may not have in regard to your respective children, it is essential that you agree on what arrangements would be in the best interests of those children in the event of your death. In the case of stepchildren, and of cohabitees, these would have to be negotiated and officially agreed before you will is drawn up.

Death can increase the bitterness in a separated family. Nancy lived with her mother after her father deserted them, and when her mother's partner Bob appeared on the scene she came to think of him as her father. Then, when she was ten years old, Nancy's mother died. Her birth father came at once to fetch her, even though Nancy pleaded to be allowed to stay with Bob. He of course had no legal rights over Nancy, and it took a great deal of negotiation in and out of court, with the help of Nancy's grandparents, to get it sorted out. Leaving such decisions until after a tragedy happens only adds to the grief of the family concerned.

It is something that grandparents too should be aware of when drafting their wills. If a child has been adopted, he is no longer related to his birth grandparent. Therefore that child would have to be specifically named in a will, not just included as a grandchild, if he is to become a beneficiary.

Seek legal advice

Of course, none of these legal concerns are straightforward. Wills can be contested, relatives can crawl out of the woodwork! And as with all the complex situations arising from the creation of a stepfamily, every problem will be slightly different. For example, whether she is divorced or a single mum, a stepmother should check if she will have to give up maintenance, child support, pension arrangements, etc. in the event of her partner's death. All such financial details must be considered. Even when you have studied the law in detail, you will still need sound legal advice (see Sources of Help).

10
The Stepchildren Talk Back

So once you have sorted out all the legal details you can concentrate on the children – learning how to have their best interests at heart. Building relationships in a stepfamily is never a quick process; there are no short cuts. Becoming a friend to a child, however, is often the way to break down many of the uncomfortable barriers that are put up when a new family is being created. It's well worth repeating that communication is the key to friendship. Letting a child talk, and listening – *really* listening, with your heart – to what they are telling you is the best way to start. If children are not talked with, not given enough information, it makes living together almost impossible.

At five years old, Rosanna was never given any explanation of her parents' behaviour:

'I didn't understand why my brother and I were going with Mum to live in Cornwall with this strange man called Giles in a small cottage. Mum said Dad was going to follow us, but he never did.' When Rosanna asked when they were going home, she was told not to be a silly child, this was her home now.

By the age of 15, she still did not know the full truth, and only learned of her parents' divorce by chance when she read one of her mother's letters from a solicitor. 'If only I had been told from the start. Naturally I had never thought of Giles as my stepfather, and though I liked him as a friend, I began to resent him being married to Mum. Why don't parents talk to their children?'

That question is constantly being asked. After all, stepfamilies would not exist without children, so it is surely a paradox that they are so seldom included in all the decisions that have to be taken before the complicated new family arrangements are made.

To anyone working with families, it soon becomes apparent that the best way to help children is to help their parents first. Is there a way to do this? Well, there is one way that seems to help all parents, especially stepparents: helping them to become aware of their child's *feelings*. Have you noticed that if you ask a parent 'How are the children?', they will tell you what they are doing, or saying, or how they are behaving – but rarely mention how they are *feeling*. 'But how can we find out?' they ask. Child therapists will confirm that this is not easy. Ask a child 'How are you feeling?' and the answer will probably be 'I don't know.' But if an adult, or older sibling, can start talking about their own feelings – 'I feel angry!' or 'I'm feeling so afraid about the future, are you?' – they can often light a spark of anger, fear or other deep emotions in a child. Out will come all the feelings that have been suppressed for a long time. Real togetherness never happens overnight; but once an adult has provided the sort of mutual help that allows a child to feel old enough to be confided in, it will give that child tremendous confidence.

Many children are now seeing their parents separating for a second or third time:

> My mum is into her third marriage now. I quite liked her second husband, but I don't want to know the others. She has had two more children and I feel sorry for them but don't want to see them. Mum has ruined my belief in family life, and Dad is not much help as he won't talk about Mum. The best thing about it all is Dad's partner, who is only two years older than me – I'm 17 now. She and I have become friends, and both agree that it's better not to get married. You cause less aggro that way.

Children learn, very young, that all relationships vary, and that lifestyles and values differ. Some youngsters are made stronger by understanding this valuable lesson, and it is reassuring to see how many children manage to come through incredibly tough experiences without losing their self-esteem. Often, it is their school that gives a child enough confidence to face adult life.

School life

The comparative security of school life – a set routine, regular hours, some form of discipline – can be the one constant in a child's life when her family situation is in turmoil. Many parents do not realize how great an impact the disrupted family life can have on their child's schooling. It is essential that they liaise with their children's teachers and exchange notes on any changes of behaviour. Lack of concentration, failing grades, disruptive behaviour or total apathy – all give teachers cause for concern. They have a huge responsibility trying to cope with the anxieties of so many of the children in their care. They know that sticking to a familiar routine can be of comfort to a child whose home life is far from stable.

Apart from being genuinely concerned for those pupils whose home situations are constantly disrupted, teachers need to have full information from the parents for legal and administrative reasons. They have to keep school records up to date; to know if a child has the same name as the parent they are living with; and who is allowed to fetch a small child from school. Most caring teachers feel that by knowing about personal situations they could never be insensitive to a child through ignorance of her background. In primary school, of course, teachers are seldom unaware of a pupil's home life: 'Tom's dad spent the night with us!'; 'I'm tired because I had to go with my brother to fetch Mum from the pub last night'. Teachers hear it all! Children, understandably, do not always tell the whole truth though: 'I didn't give my teacher Mum's new name because I didn't want mine to be different.' On the other hand, a child may feel her teacher is the only person she can confide in: 'I told my teacher when Dad was sent to prison because I had no one else to talk to.'

Mothers, especially stepmothers, are often reluctant to ask for help. They feel they have failed if they cannot control the children. This is when a head teacher can sometimes suggest a session with the educational psychologist, explaining that it would be in the interest of the child. The basic rule for parents is that the child's feelings should be paramount. Sometimes it is a teacher who will explain to a child's parents what those feelings are, and surprise them with the child's wishes – usually the opposite of what the parents have assumed them to be: 'Mum told my teacher that I wanted to live with her when she moved in with her boyfriend, but she had never even asked me! I actually wanted desperately to live with Dad and my brother.'

We all know how manipulative children can be. A great deal of guilt is around during and after separation and remarriage, and the stepchildren know this! Just as they do during a divorce or bereavement, they can use the family upheaval as an excuse to act as they please, as well as drawing attention to themselves – 'I feel too sad to go to school today'; 'We can't go to football now Dad isn't here to come with us'. They can play on a parent's or grandparent's sympathy, and for an inexperienced stepparent it can be a clever, if cruel, device. Eventually you will have to let them know that certain behaviours are not tolerated in your house!

Seeking help

But how can you, as a stepparent, tell if a child is simply playing you up or genuinely in need of help – possibly professional help? Children often hide their anxieties and I've heard adults say, 'Oh, they are not affected at all, we get on famously!' Then, when their backs are turned, the children will shake their heads in despair: 'That's what they think!'

Small children will show emotional and physical symptoms that are not so hard to pick up. Some revert to baby habits such as bedwetting, whining and clinging behaviour, refusing food and not sleeping. Extra loving care and attention will usually solve the problem, given time and patience. Older schoolchildren may develop high temperatures, rashes or stomach upsets – some develop a stammer, or become sullen and aggressive. If you suspect any such behavioural patterns are not normal, then seek advice. Your family doctor is usually the best person to consult as he will be able to refer you to a local child guidance clinic. The children may refuse to attend, or at least grumble at you for suggesting there is anything wrong with them, but eventually they will see that you care about them and want to help. Don't hesitate to contact members of the extended family if relationships are amicable – grandparents who are familiar to a child can often offer emotional and practical help, and reassure her that not everything in her life has changed.

'My grandfather is my best friend,' said one twelve-year-old boy after both his parents had remarried. 'He is showing me how to react to trouble – especially to violence from my stepfather. I know now how to listen and respond to people who disagree with me, though it's hard at times. I wish my parents could learn this too.' A valuable lesson in 'Relationships' – a subject that might well be added to the three Rs in every school curriculum.

One teacher told me of a boy in middle school who never got his homework book signed by his parent:

> He told me that his dad didn't live with him any more, his stepparent refused to help me, and his mum was too busy with her new baby. I suggested that he phone his dad who used to help him, but the next day the boy told me that his dad's new partner answered the phone and told him to stop being a nuisance. I can only try to give that child extra help in class, but I doubt if either of his parents will turn up to Parents' Evening.

Some parents are appalled at the thought of such a thing as professional help – either for themselves, their partners, or their children. Of course, if there is violence or abuse in the family, no one must ever hesitate to seek help. You may well feel that you need help for yourself – and there is plenty of support on offer today. Never feel that because you are not a natural parent that organizations such as Parentline Plus can't help you. Parents today include foster parents, adoptive parents, grandparents and stepparents. There are parenting (and even grandparenting!) courses available, which can give great confidence to stepparents who feel they are failing in their new role. If it is a case of a child being excessively disruptive, or you suspect he is using drugs, it is wise to find a child therapist. Family counselling can often be very therapeutic for a family in crisis, but of course it is not always possible to get every member to attend! There are more and more self-help groups starting up all over the country, and talking with families in the same situation as yourself can often be a great help – a kind of mutual counselling service. Your doctor's surgery, the Citizens' Advice Bureau, your church, or your child's school, may all have a list of groups in your neighbourhood.

Stepfamilies at their best

Many people assume that stepfamilies, because they are made up from separated families, or 'broken' families as some people like to call them, must always remain under that label. Broken. But as one 11-year-old boy expressed it:

I've never felt abandoned by my parents. OK, Dad and Mum divorced, and we all hated that at the time even though they talked openly about it with us. But we still see both of them and their new partners are pretty good to me and my brothers – we have what my gran calls a stable home life. I know some of our teachers thought because we're from a stepfamily we'd be stupid, but I don't know why, it doesn't seem fair. My best friend lives with both his natural parents and has a horrid time – they're always fighting and moving house and I guess it's far from stable. We know how lucky we are.

This, clearly, is stepparenting at its best.

How sad for children and their parents that they hear so much talk about families living and growing up in inferior situations. Everyone knows the statistics on stepfather violence, even murder, and the media-covered instances of stepmother cruelty. But there are good and bad characters in every group of people. And just because stepfamilies are more complex than most, in many cases this does not mean that they are less well adjusted, or that they have less to offer their children.

A stepfather of ten years' standing was heard to say: 'We both have new partners, and now care deeply for each other's children. We have fulfilled lives.'

One teenage girl who has had a natural mother and father, two stepmothers and one stepfather, was equally comforting in her views on family life: 'Because both my parents love me, I have never felt deprived in any way. Sad at times, yes, but who isn't?'

Children can be more philosophical than adults realize. Jamie is only seven, but he summed up his life in a stepfamily with a smile: 'I guess the whole thing is OK when you get used to it.'

One stepfamily confirmed the long-held theory that laughter can be the best medicine for all sorts of problems:

> Alec and his two sons, each one born from a different mother, married Prue who has a son and two daughters who are the children of Thomas. Alec's two former wives have remarried as has Thomas, so that the number of children between all of them is now 12. At first, Alec's and Prue's children were extremely wary of each other. As one of them said: 'We don't even know these kids, it's crazy having to live with them!'

Then one day the eldest boy began to question why they should be called stepbrothers and stepsisters, and one of Prue's daughters told him to look the words up in the dictionary. The first definition they found was, 'Step: the single movement of raising one foot and putting it down in another spot.' Then they read out, 'in step', 'out of step', 'watch one's step'. The list went on and soon the whole family joined in. Prue found that a step could mean 'a stage in a process', which she thought described a stepfamily. 'And what about "step by step" meaning gradually?' asked Alec. The girls began to giggle when they found 'step down, meaning to take a lesser position'. But then they found 'step meaning relationship through the remarriage of a parent rather than by blood'. That was when the laughter started: 'At least there's no blood around – *yet*!'

When they all found there was humour in their situation as well as anxiety, the atmosphere in that household relaxed. The parents realized, for the first time, that they had all joined in the dictionary game together – and that was to be the key to their continued success as a family. They spent time together. Days would go by, weeks sometimes, when they were all busy with their own affairs – school, work, friends, and of course visiting their other families – but whenever possible they planned outings, meals, or just played some childish game together as a family.

The challenges of stepparenting can be enormous, but what of the rewards? Surely not all families can achieve such togetherness?

One woman said: 'I often feel I *can't* ever be friends with, let alone love, my partner's children. They're selfish and rude, noisy and wilful. And then one day they appear with their arms full of flowers for me, or I catch sight of them gently helping my own little girl to play on her swing, and my heart misses a beat. I know I can't *not* love them!'

All happiness, all feelings of friendship and love, come in such fleeting moments when we least expect them. Don't miss them.

Sources of Help

Child and Family Guidance Clinics
Ask your GP or local Citizens' Advice Bureau for your nearest Clinic.

Family Mediators Association
020 7881 9400
Will provide names of family mediators in your area.

Families Need Fathers
134 Curtain Road
London EC2A 3AR
020 7613 5060
Keeping children and parents in contact.

Home Start UK
2 Salisbury Road
Leicester LE1 7QR
0116 233 9955
Support for young families in their own homes. Branches throughout the country.

National Association of Citizens' Advice Bureaux
Citizens' Advice Bureaux will offer advice, useful addresses, and further sources of help. Your nearest branch will be listed in the local telephone directory.

Parentline Plus
520 Highgate Studios
53–79 Highgate Road
Kentish Town
London NW5 1TL
020 7284 5500
Incorporates the National Stepfamily Association, Parent Network, and Parentline.
Free confidential helpline: 0808 800 2222

SOURCES OF HELP

Relate
Head Office
Herbert Gray College
Little Church Street
Rugby CV21 3AP
01788 573241

Solicitors Family Law Association (SFLA)
PO Box 302
Orpington
Kent BR6 8QX
01689 850227
Will provide lists of skilled solicitors in your area.

The Tavistock Clinic
College Crescent
120 Belsize Lane
London NW3 5BA
020 7435 7111
NHS out-patient clinic which promotes the mental health of families. Contact the Child and Family Department (up to age 13) Mon–Fri. For the Adolescent Department (ages 14–21), phone 020 7447 3714. Adolescents over 16 (and up to age 30) can phone or write to the Young People's Consultation Service for an appointment on 020 7447 3787. This is a self-referral service which provides a brief period of counselling (four sessions).

Further Reading

Barnes, Gill Gorell, *Family Therapy in Changing Times*, Macmillan, 1998.
Barnes, Gill Gorell, Thompson, Paul, Daniel, Gwyn and Burchardt, Natasha, *Growing up in Stepfamilies*, Oxford University Press, 1997.
Batchelor, Jane, Dimmock, Brian, and Smith, Donna, *Understanding Stepfamilies*, Stepfamily Publications (from Stepfamily Telephone Counselling Service).
Eckler, James D., *Step-by-Step Parenting*, Betterway Books, 1993.
Fowler, Deborah, *Loving other People's Children*, Hodder & Stoughton, 1992.
Hayman, Suzie, *The Relate Guide to Second Families*, Vermilion, 1997.
Newman, Margaret, *Stepfamily Realities*, New Harbinger Publications, California, 1994.
Norwood, Perdita Kirkness, with Wingender, Teri, *The Enlightened Stepmother*, Avon Books Inc., New York, 1999.
Trollope, Joanna, *Other People's Children*, Bloomsbury, 1998.
Visher, Emily B., PhD and Visher, John S., MD, *How to Win as a Stepfamily*, Brunner/Mazel, New York, 1982.

Books for Children

Braithwaite, Althea, *My Two Families*, A & C Black, 1996.
Broere, Rien, *You Will Always Be My Dad*, Evans Brothers, 1997.
Bryant-Mole, Karen, *Splitting Up*, Wayland, 1992.
Burrett, Jill, *But I Want to Stay with You*, Simon & Schuster, 1999.
Fine, Anne, *Goggle-Eyes*, Hamish Hamilton, 1989 (middle school upwards).
Hunter, Rebecca, *My New Dad*, Evans Brothers, 2000.
Johnson, Julie, *How Do I Feel about My Stepfamily?*, Franklin Watts, 1997 (primary).
Murphy, Jill, *Worlds Apart*, Walker Books, 1988 (age 11 upwards).
Wilson, Jacqueline, *The Suitcase Kid*, Doubleday, 1992.

Index

Abduction: of children 21; parents fighting for contact 54, 76, 91, 97
adoption 100–2
anger 54–7

bereavement 25, 32, 35, 38–40, 103
biological parents 2, 20–2, 89; suffering jealousy 50–1

Child Support Agency 98–100
Children Act 1989 86, 95–6, 97
Children, listening to 18–19, 105–6

discipline 63–6, 68
divorce: between grandparents 88; effect on children 2, 13–14, 83

ex-partners 6–7, 37, 55, 88–93; see also part-time stepparents

family therapists 14, 38, 55–7, 64, 69, 80, 106, 108
finance, maintenance payments 54, 99, 103

grandparents 80, 83–7, 108; step-grandparents 87–8
guidelines: for stepchildren 67; for stepparents 67
guilt 48–9

homes: living in two 27; sharing 28, 35, 62–4

jealousy 10, 28, 49–53, 72–3

laughter, as therapy 110–11
legal matters 95–103; wills 102–3
lifestyles, differing 59–63

parental responsibility: 86, 90, 96–8
parents: advice from therapists 57, 109; parenting courses 79; parental alienation syndrome 92–3
part-time stepparents 26–9
physical reactions: in children 49, 56, 108; therapeutic activities 56
problems: behavioural 23, 28, 30, 42, 63–6, 68–9; emotional 30, 75–6; sexual 75–81

rejection: fear of 44; of relatives 98, 83–5
resentment 14, 38, 42, 53–4

school 106–8; educational psychologists 107, 109; teachers 107
second marriages: divided loyalties 44, 47–8; starting a second family 52, 71–4, 88; weddings 43–6
stepchildren: first meeting with 15–18; half-brothers and sisters 22, 44, 52, 74; step-siblings 51–3, 78
stepfathers 5–6; getting it right 21, 61, 109–11; living away from their children 23–4, 26, 76–7; with no children of their own 7–9, 37–8, 68–9
stepmothers 3–5, 24; getting it right 42, 61, 109–11; with no children of their own 8, 17–18, 36–37, 66

talking: with a partner 40–1; with children 13–15, 18–20, 22, 40–1
teenagers 29, 45, 74–81
tension, in stepfamilies 25, 32, 61

visiting, by children 6, 23–5, 26–8, 50, 65–6, 75, 93; by parents 52–4, 89–90, 91–2